Motivating Marvin:
Helping Your Bright
Underachiever Succeed in School

Motivating Marvin:
Helping Your Bright Underachiever Succeed in School

Steven G. Gray, Ph.D., A.B.Pd.N.

Photography by Sandi Evans
Illustrations by Tricia Lambert

Gray Neuropsychology Associates, Inc.
Dallas, Texas
Colorado Springs, Colorado

MOTIVATING MARVIN: HELPING YOUR BRIGHT UNDERACHIEVER
SUCCEED IN SCHOOL

Published by Living Water Press
Colorado Springs, Colorado
For Permission/Information Address: 1840 Deer Creek Road, Suite 103
                                          Monument, CO 80132
e-mail: gray.matter@mindspring.com   Phone: 719.487.1760
www.grayneuro.com   Fax: 719.487.1755

All Scripture references, unless otherwise noted, are taken from the *New American Standard Bible*, © 1960, 1962, 1963, 1968, 1971, 1972, 1973, 1975, 1977, 1995 by The Lockman Foundation. Used by permission. (www.Lockman.org)

The Message by Eugene H. Peterson, copyright © 1993, 1994, 1995, 1996, 2000, 2001, 2002. Used by permission of NavPress Publishing Group. All rights reserved.

Library of Congress Control Number: 2004091698
Cataloging-in-Publication Data
Gray, Steven G., 1953 –
Motivating Marvin: helping your bright underachiever succeed in school

Includes biographical references and index
1. Underachievers   2. Academic achievement   3. Parenting
4. Learning difficulties   5. Psychology and psychiatry
I. Gray, Steven.   II. Title.

ISBN: 0-9746412-1-9

Printed in the United States of America

Table of Contents

Part V Managing Marvin

Part VI Marvin Under the Microscope

Part VII End Notes

Acknowledgements

To my Lord and Savior, Jesus Christ, who has afforded me countless blessings.

To my lovely wife, Debbi, who has loved and supported me for 23 years.

To my son, Forrest, of whom I am very proud.

To my late father and mother, Ed and Juanita Gray, who provided me with a loving, supportive home.

To my sister, Pam, who has always been a huge encouragement to me.

To my aunt, Allene Gray, who instilled in me a love of learning.

To Dr. Bill Whitehouse, cousin, surrogate uncle, and world-class role model.

To Jean LaPrade, teacher extraordinaire, who helped foster in me what it takes to complete a project.

To the late Bryan Duff, who engendered in me a love of writing.

To Howard Hughes, who believed in me.

To Dr. Jack Dial, good friend and invaluable mentor.

To Dr. Charles Golden, who motivated me.

To Dan McGee, long-time friend and private practice role model.

To Tricia Lambert, whose research efforts and many valuable suggestions allowed this book to become reality.

Introduction

Few situations I am asked to deal with rival the frustration of having an intelligent yet academically underachieving young person in the home. For you as a parent, attempting to get your bright kiddo to succeed in school – when he or she possesses not the remotest interest in doing so – is tantamount to trying to hammer a limp noodle through a piece of sheet rock.

Over the years, in dealing with the bright academic underachiever, I have learned much via trial and error, in terms of what works and what doesn't. A significant portion of my learning comes from Dr. Sylvia Rimm, with whom I had the fortune of spending a week's worth of training, back in the early 90s up in her home state of Wisconsin.

If this book can add a scintilla to Dr. Rimm's important writings within the realm of treating the bright underachiever, I'll be very pleased. Although I may bring a bit of a different outlook to her seminal work on the topic, my perspectives are very much in tune with hers.

I also am grateful to the families I've seen over the past 22 years, who have added immeasurably to my knowledge and understanding of what it takes to rectify the myriad of underachieving "Marvins" we as parents are entrusted to raise. It really is true that for clinicians only so much can be learned, of a practical nature, in graduate school. Getting down and dirty in the trenches with real people hampered by real problems is what it takes.

Finally, many times over the years, parents of academic underachievers have asked me for something in writing that could serve as a tangible guide for them in dealing with their own incredibly frustrating Marvin. My prayer is that this book scratches that itch.

Steven Gray, Ph.D.
Colorado Springs, Colorado
September 2004

Motivating Marvin

Part I

Matriculation for Marvin

Chapter 1

How Important, Really, *Is* School?

As adults, most of us have jobs. Except for me. The last *real* job I had was in 1984 – 20 years ago at the time of this writing. I had finished up my internship at the University of Nebraska Medical Center. Upon leaving Omaha – a great city, by the way, my wife and I moved to Arlington, Texas where I began a year of post-doctoral training at Metro Counseling Associates. MCA was a private outpatient Christian mental health clinic, led by Drs. Dan McGee and Ewing Cooley. Ever since the one year salaried position that I had there, I have been *unemployed*.

Only private practice.

And private practice – with all its vicissitudes, can hardly count as a real/honest-to-goodness job, I'm afraid. But, forgive me. My first of what will be several digressions within the course of this book.

O.K. Back on task now. As to the value of education, I look at school as a youth's *job*.

So, yeah, I think academics are important.

A child or teen *should* do her best in school. Just as an adult should do his best on the job.

Having said that, I don't think it's God's will that every child make straight-A's. Trite as it sounds, each young person should do her best within the school milieu. If that equates out to a solid B student, fine. If it's consistent C's – that's O.K. too. But her BEST.

As parents, if the truth be known, we'd all like our kids to make the Honor Roll every 6 weeks. Living through our offspring, some might claim. Nevertheless, living *through* our youth is something we all as parents have to battle.

Ever read the Christmas cards some folks send out? You know, the ones with the printed narratives regarding their families? Most are rife with all manner of references to what their kids have achieved over the past 12 months. Hey, it's human nature for us to be proud of our children's accomplishments. At times though such can take on a life of its own – with us living vicariously via our offspring...By the way, have I mentioned how my son did recently on his...Sorry.

Anyway, for Christians, it all boils down to calling. God's calling. Vocation is actually derived from the Latin root, *vocare*: to call. God, you see, has a blueprint, or calling, for each of us.

> *"For I know the plans that I have for you," declares the Lord, "plans for welfare and not for calamity, to give you a future and a hope."* Jeremiah 29:11

I recall as a young teenager – age 13ish, I was obsessed with what my vocation (God's plan for me) was to be. Very few days passed by, from early adolescence, wherein I failed to specifically ask God via prayer what he wanted me to be when I grew up. It never occurred to me that God *didn't* have a roadmap for my life.

Well, I continued praying and seeking wise counsel. For years. In fact, roughly the next 8 years, from 1966 until late 1974, age 21. Age 21½, to be exact – November of 1974.

Prior to 11/74 (the first semester during my senior year of college) not only did I pray, but I listened. To others in various occupations: Law, Medicine, Theology. All three seemed to be possibilities for me.

Having emerged from an extended family top-heavy with attorneys, law school was a front-burner push. In fact, my mother – quite plainly – opined that I should become a lawyer. And, I had any number of excellent attorney role-models (both family and non-family) to watch. Growing up in the rural small town of Cleburne, Texas – 30 miles south of Fort Worth – I had my uncle, Gean Turner, a gifted litigator. There was also an affable and astute Christian man at my church, Bob Mahanay – a local Cleburne attorney – whom I admired very much.

However, on the very street (Forrest Avenue) in Cleburne where I grew up – actually only one block north – was another unbelievable role model, Dr. Bill Whitehouse. Bill was my cousin (and surrogate uncle, actually), a thoracic surgeon. Plus, the inner workings of the human body interested me a great deal. So, Medicine was another logical possibility for me.

On the other hand, I crossed paths with some excellent theologians as well, growing up in First Baptist Church of Cleburne. For example, there was my senior pastor during high school, Lou Brown. Also of significant impact to me were interims: Dr. Bill Hendricks, as well as Dr. Huber Drumwright, whom I furthermore greatly admired. Moreover, youth ministers, David LeGrand and Dr. Tom Nettles, mentored and befriended me during my high school and college years. Besides, there was fascination with the Word of God. So, why not a seminary education?

By the time I arrived at Baylor, the field of Psychology – specifically Christian Psychology – had begun to interest me. The integration of Biblical teachings with the science of human behavior was taking on roots of intrigue for me.

Making a long story painful, I was still – at the onset of my senior year in college – fairly frustrated and confused as to what my vocation was to be. Waiting on the Lord is not easy for a Choleric (see Chapter 6).

Then, in November of 1974 – my senior year at Baylor – I vividly recall one particular evening – studying at the library. (Such is not to be confused with *The Library*, a circa 1970s bar on 5th Street, only blocks from campus. I'm talking the **Moody** Library, for you Baylor Bears out there.)

Anyway, as I was sitting in a study carrel at Moody, a very pronounced countenance suddenly came over me. I had no doubt God was internally whispering to me: "Steve, you are to pursue Christian Psychology..."

Wow! After years of prayer, deliberation, and seeking out wise counsel – the Holy Spirit finally spoke to me on the issue of vocation – *my* vocation!

I soon thereafter eagerly proceeded back to my modest Waco abode near campus (roommates: Rick Long, James McDougald, and David Stricklin). As I entered Flagship Apartments #222, there was David – fellow Cleburnite and my best friend from childhood – sitting on his bed, studying. I'll never forget my verbatim – "Dave, I *know* what I'm supposed to do!" I then informed him of my revelation experience at the library.

So, what does this personal experience of mine have to do with the price of peas in Peru? Simply to illustrate that God indeed does honor consistent prayer, as well as a sincere desire to know Him.

However, what if – during my school years, growing up – I'd not been motivated to study hard and do my best within the classroom? Well, I likely would have painted myself into an academic corner. That is, having not done my best in school, God's plan for my life might well have been thwarted.

See, it's not necessarily about making the Honor Roll time after time, or ultimately getting into Harvard. It's about *doing your best*. Or, within the context of this book, it's about us helping our kids do their best in school. Why? So God's blue-print for our son or daughter's vocational life is not impeded – painted into the proverbial corner as it were.

My vow with this book is to do everything I can to help you help your child do his best in the classroom.

Ready to come along? O.K., let's motivate Marvin.

Motivating Marvin

Part II

Making Sense of Marvin's Underachievement

Chapter 2

The Neuropsychologic Evaluation

First of all, what about flushing out any collateral complicating childhood/adolescent syndromes which might otherwise be gunking up Marvin's academic progress? Well, in my case, I use a neuropsychologic (NP) battery of 23 procedures, each measuring different brain regions/functions.

Via the analysis of these psychometric tests/data for Marvin, and the composite picture they create, I can get an excellent idea of any *gar-bagé* root causes entangling Marvin. By *gar-bagé* root causes, I mean such syndromes as: ADHD, LDs, masked depression, anxiety factors, etc. The value of differential diagnosis in the treatment of academic underachievement is huge (Mandel & Marcus, 1988).

The purpose of these various tests is aimed at discovering what manner of brain-based disturbance might be unwittingly contributing to any refuse entangling the goal of academic success for our man, Marvin.

While many of the Dependent Underachiever (DU) youth I see have similar **symptoms**, does that mean they all have the same underlying diagnoses (i.e., underlying *gar-bagé*)? Unfortunately, no. The endemic mystery in working with young persons is first determining what is going on with that particular youth – be it a child or teen.

In fact, give me ten 13 year-olds – with identical symptom pictures – and I can hand you back ten different constellations of underlying root causes. For one kiddo, it might be a Tex-Mex combo plate of LD, ADHD, and covert depression. For another, it could be a cocktail

16

of: anxiety, a nasty Narcissistic trait, and unresolved anger. For yet another, we might simply be looking at an immature Sanguine teen who has yet to decide that academic excellence should be high on her food chain of priorities.

The usual common denominator though with the youth I see – who are struggling in school – is that most possess the DU designation, along with other accompanying *gar-bagé* syndromes, rendering the academic mayhem infinitely more difficult to nuke. Well, without a thorough NP exam, we simply don't know **what** the heck is tripping these kiddoes up.

It's akin to one of the corny jokes my old friend, Dale Hannah of Cleburne, Texas routinely tells. One such misguided jocular account of his pertains to the legendary yet fictitious *Heck-ow-ie* Indians. The tribe is constantly lost, frequently posing the question: "Where the *Heck-ow-ie*?!!"

Well, if we try treating all young persons the same, we shoot ourselves (along with them and their parents) in the foot. We're constantly trying to find out *where the heck **are** we.*

So, how do I help Marvin and his parents attack a problem (in this case, an academic performance resting firmly in the toilet) if we don't have a clear idea as to the actual *source* of the meltdown? Answer: we can't!

Thus, without a comprehensive NP evaluation, we are only able to see – from the surface of the water – the tip of the iceberg. That is – the youth's presenting problems (bad grades, poor study habits, oppositionalism, etc). However, as the Captain of *The Titanic* can ably attest, the bulk of the iceberg lies underneath the waterline. The NP exam, then, allows us to clearly examine what is indeed beneath surface eye-level. To borrow from an old saying: *If we know our enemy, we can attack.*

The good news here is that DU youth, in the vast majority of instances, **can** be helped – even if we are talking major academic crash-and-burn.

The first trick though is finding out for Marvin precisely what sort of *gar-bagé* needs to be cleaned out. The thoroughness of the NP evaluation ensures we don't just scoop a little off the surface (a la the use of a simplistic parent/teacher checklist or two, then go to the house). Thus, we (i.e., I and the parents) must first do our homework regarding Marvin.

Anyway, once the tests are completed, I score and analyze the results. It's important that the ensuing data are fully understood in light of: (1) my eye-ball observations of Marvin; along with (2) Marvin's overall background. You, the parents, have already given me: medical history, his vegetative signs (i.e., wake/sleep cycle, appetite), academic habits, interpersonal skills, and so forth. All are vital in helping to determine the root causes of **Marvin's** scholastic underachievement.

It takes 10 to 14 calendar days after the date of testing for all results and findings to be assayed. In addition, a thorough report detailing Marvin's presenting problems, history, psychometric data, conclusions, diagnoses, and recommendations is generated (upon request).

The next phase is the feedback session. Here, I go over with you the test findings and recommendations. We take our time. I answer your questions. We carefully talk through the underlying root causes for Marvin's struggles. Then, we slowly work our way through the pros and cons for the entire laundry list of tenable recommendations. (See the rest of this book for the most common options for helping Marvin.)

My goal and expectation are that your youth *will* find light at the end of the tunnel – God willing. I am very blessed and humbled, inasmuch as my calling has been to help young people find theirs. And you'd be surprised how many "hopeless" kiddoes end up doing just that!

But first we need a blueprint. The NP exam *is* that blueprint.

Chapter 3

The ADHD Weighting Scale

You may have heard it said, "There *is* no test for ADHD."
True and not true.

While there's no **one** measure capable of diagnosing ADHD, a battery of such tests can pinpoint the disorder quite well – via an ADHD Weighting Scale. From years of working with kiddoes, making careful observations, I fumbled upon the development of such. The tool uses a cluster of specific attention-sensitive tests. Taken together, this psychometric cornucopia can depict whether or not ADHD is hindering Marvin in the quest for academic achiever status.

Basically, what we have here is a mini-battery of attention-sensitive tests, all placed on the Attention Deficit Hyperactivity Weighting Scale (Gray, 1996). The results provide a quantifiable pro-file of attention/concentration, from which a very good picture of a youth's ADHD status can be deduced. As I stated earlier, we can't hang our hat on any *single* measure for this disorder.

Some of the behaviors typically associated with ADHD can actu-ally stem from a variety of sources: childhood depression/anxiety, a Choleric temperament (see Chapter 6), etc. But if we just rear back and call Marvin ADHD, based solely on his outward *behavior* – or from a checklist filled out by Mom or Teacher, we do the kiddo a huge disser-vice.

Moreover, I can't **tell** you how many youth I've seen who have had all manner of behavioral syndromes going on below the waterline, including ADHD – wherein the only disorder on the tip of the iceberg –

able to be seen with the naked eye, was an obvious ADHD. Well, if we only treat the ADHD – and none of the other underlying root causes of the academic/behavioral problems hampering Marvin, he continues

Attention Deficit Hyperactivity Weighting Scale
(Marvin's Sample)*

MODALITY	WEIGHTING	MODALITY	WEIGHTING
TESTING SESSION		**GORDON**	
Fidgets/Impulsive	2	Delay	1
Motoric Over-Activity	6	Vigilance	1
Poor Attention	3	Distractibility	1
SCHOOL SETTING		Commission Errors	3*
Fidgets/Impulsive	2*	**TAD**	
Motoric Over-Activity	5	Quiet	2
Poor Attention	2*	Distractibility	2*
PIC		**STROOP**	
ADHD: $\geq$ 90	2*	Word	1
80-90		Color	1
LITTAUER		Color-Word	1
Primary Sanguine	3	**SPEECH SOUNDS**	
Secondary Sanguine	2*	Distractibility	2
WISC-III		**SEASHORE RHYTHM**	
Arithmetic	1	Distractibility	2*
Digit Span	1*	**REITAN-KLOVE**	
Coding	1	Distractibility	1
Picture Completion	1	Distractibility	1
		TOTAL	**16**

*The numbers above reveal ADHD–specific tests which Marvin (age 13) had difficulty with.

RAW SCORE			RANGE
0	—	12	= WNL
13	—	**16**	= **Mild Range**
17	—	20	= Moderate Range
21	—	↑	= Severe Range

*Scores > 12 are positive for ADHD

Figure 3.1 Attention Hyperactivity Weighting Scale

to struggle. This is precisely why a thorough NP evaluation is so crucial. The ADHD Weighting Scale is part of the comprehensive NP exam (Gray, 2004).

In conclusion, ADHD is a fairly common underlying root cause – or **contributing** root cause – as to why DUs remain DUs. Hence, this is the reason I am devoting a short chapter to ADHD. We either need to rule in or rule out this widely misunderstood syndrome for Marvin.

Chapter 4

Learning Disabilities

What about Learning Disabilities? Well, LDs can be subtle, or not so subtle. Either way, if Marvin is wrestling with an LD, we need to know about it. Moreover, there is an important distinction to make within this syndrome: *neurologic* and *functional*.

A neurologic LD is due to a physiologic anomaly affecting the brain. The hard-wiring is somehow slightly askew – oftentimes due to nothing more than pure genetics.

Traumatic brain injuries however can also produce a neurologic LD, as can in utero drug/alcohol exposure. Another form of LD is the Non-verbal Learning Disability (discussed below).

For those of you interested in discovering more about neurologic LDs, see Walbrown & Walbrown's (1990) *So Your Child Has a Learning Problem: Now What?* Additionally, Federici (1998) has an excellent overview of LDs in Chapter 3 of his book, *Help for the Hopeless Child*.

A functional Learning Disability, on the other hand – while sharing many of the same outward appearances as a neurologic LD (e.g., Marvin can't read very well, do simple long division, etc) – is due to very different root causes. Part of the reality for us who use psychologic and neuropsychologic data is that we can't always take such at *face value*. I am unable to accurately assess all the numbers I get from psychometric data, without marrying them to Marvin's history/past circumstances, as well as obtaining a thorough understanding of the subtleties inherent in each test I give him. More about this in a moment.

Woodcock-Johnson Revised

One of the assessment tools I use in determining whether Marvin possesses a functional or neurologic LD is the Woodcock Johnson-Revised (WJ-R). The WJ-R gives me a detailed analysis of academic skills (and sometimes helps tell me how *bright* Marvin really is as well).

The WJ-R measures: reading, math, and writing skills (*the Three R's*). I then compare Marvin's scores against his actual grade placement.

When a kiddo receives a low score on any WJ-R subtest, it's imperative to know how to interpret the results. For example, my job is to determine whether a low phonics score is a sign of a phonics-based LD, or if such is simply the result of Marvin having been immersed in a *Whole Language* learning system year after year at school – an educational approach which basically omits the teaching of old-fashioned phonics.

Gray Writing Samples Test

Another tool I use to augment the WJ-R's written language assessment is the Gray Writing Samples Test (Gray, 1994). Here, we present two action pictures to Marvin, one at a time. He can write whatever brief story his little heart desires, regarding each scene.

For young children, we simply dictate the 26 letters of the English alphabet (out of sequence) for the kiddo to produce on a piece of paper. If he is unable to write the letters via dictation, we allow him to simply copy them one at a time. So, the Gray Writing Samples Test (GWST) is individually tailored to the age and writing skill competency of a specific youngster.

The GWST can also reveal Graphic Dyspraxia (an impairment in the quality of printing/cursive), or Dyslexia (brain-based difficulties in reading and/or writing – substituting "d"s for "b"s, improper usage of capital letters, extremely poor spelling, incorrect verb usage, etc).

Non-verbal Learning Disabilities

A Non-verbal Learning Disability (NLD) is a neurologic condition generally thought to emanate from the right cerebral hemisphere. Reception and processing of nonverbal stimuli are problematic (Rourke, 1995). Children with NLD are thought to frequently *struggle* with:

> - motor coordination/balance
> - visual-spatial skills
> - social judgment – involving the discombobulation of interpersonal cues given off by others

Youth with NLD are, on the other hand, thought to have the following *strengths*:

> - precocious speech and vocabulary development
> - robust rote memory skills
> - early development of reading/spelling
> - verbal eloquence
> - strong auditory retention

Bottom line, another purpose of a comprehensive NP evaluation is to determine whether a functional LD, or a neurologic LD/NLD is present for Marvin, serving to further complicate his DU status.

Learning Styles

Not to be confused with Learning Disabilities, Learning Styles (LSs) have to do with the manner in which young people (and to a great extent older persons) best *take in* information. Some of us for example are auditory learners. Some of us are visual learners. Yet others are tactile (touch) learners.

From my readings, there is no question but what LSs overlap – to a degree at least – with God-given temperament. For example, many persons who appear to be primarily auditory learners tend to be Sanguines (see Chapter 6). On the other hand, it seems to me that many primarily Melancholic temperaments gravitate more toward the visual learning realm. Clearly however there are exceptions. To muddy the waters even more, very few individuals are solely auditory, or solely visual for example, in their LS. Almost all of us possess an admixture of auditory, visual, tactile, etc.

Quite a bit has been written about LSs. Thus, if LS is an aspect you desire to study, consider Gregorc's (1982) *An Adult's Guide to Style*, or Tobias' (1996) *Every Child Can Succeed.*

Chapter 5

Realistic Academic Expectations

Oftentimes parents will come in and say, "Well, Marvin is bright, but he's flunking everything. While we know he can do a lot better than straight F's, what grades *should* he be making? A's and B's? Solid B's? Straight A's?"

This is of course a very valid question. I tell Marvin's parents, "Once we get the results back from his NP exam, we'll know exactly what is realistic to expect from him, grade-wise."

For example, when the NP data are in, it may well be that a mild ADHD is present. Perhaps a subtle atypical (covert) depression is on Marvin's plate. Or, maybe both.

The main idea to be grasped is this: whatever's going on with Marvin, once it's known specifically what he's up against, we can act. He may simply be a strong-willed Choleric/immature young man – and nothing else. But regardless, as I said earlier, once we know the enemy, we can formulate a tailored battle plan – with huge odds of success, in my experience.

Remember, what is my general expectation for Marvin? That he do his best – whatever that turns out to be – with us as parents regarding school as Marvin's *job*. Remember, as adults, we all have jobs. Some of us are in sales. Some are plumbers. Some are stay-at-home moms. Others attorneys. But we all have a job. And it's expected that we do our best there.

It's no different with Marvin and academics. School is his job, and I expect him to do his best. Not necessarily right away. That would be an unrealistic expectation. But down the road a bit, after we have a chance to tweak under his hood, I expect him to do his best.

So, dear parents, read on!

Motivating Marvin

Part III

Marvin's Modus Operandi

Chapter 6

Marvin's Personality Temperament

Human temperament is thought to be chiefly derived from God-given genetics, plus the first 6 years of life experiences. Most experts on the topic classify people according to four basic personality groupings. Much of the following material is taken from the work of Tim LaHaye, along with Florence and Fred Littauer. All are Christian speakers/writers who have done many seminars and written profusely within this area (LaHaye, 1993; Littauer, 1992).

Another notable Christian author/speaker of our day, Gary Smalley (Smalley, 1990), uses the same temperament groupings as does LaHaye and the Littauers; he simply employs different names for them (discussed below).

The four temperaments are: *Choleric, Sanguine, Melancholy*, and *Phlegmatic*. I use a test called the *Personality Profile*, consisting of 40 fill-in-the blank choices, developed by the Littauers (Littauer, 1983). This instrument helps identify Marvin's primary and secondary temperaments. It's typically completed by the young person's parents.

In my opinion, the aspect of temperament – via getting to know the underachieving Marvin – is a good way to start off. You *realize* Marvin is bright; however, his grades aren't anywhere remotely within the same cosmos as his potential. Anyway, I like to begin by looking at the personality temperament. (To check out Marvin's personality temperament, see Chapter 32.)

First, it's widely accepted that every human being possesses a **primary** temperament, and a **secondary** temperament. The two on the left of Figure 6.1 below (Sanguine and Choleric) are considered to be the extroverted temperament types. The two on the right are the introverted types (Melancholy and Phlegmatic).

E X T R O V E R T	Sanguine	Melancholy	I N T R O V E R T
	Choleric	Phlegmatic	

Figure 6.1 The Four Personality Temperaments

We have all known people who are very extroverted – effervescent, bubbly, social. And the vast majority have always been that way. No one *taught* them how to be outgoing (provided they are true extroverts).

Conversely, we've all been acquainted with persons who are shy, retiring, reticent. And, no one taught them to be introverts. They didn't attend a weekly Introversion Class at the local YMCA every Thursday night during 3rd grade. Their brains have – in the main – been hardwired by God in such fashion (also allowing for the effects of the first 6 years of life experiences).

Consider babies smack dab out of the womb. You see some – right off the bat – who are affectionate, cooey, eat everything you give them straight from the vine, and sleep through the night. Just real cuddle-buns.

You also of course see children who come into the world colicky. They don't want to be touched too much. They cry a lot. They don't sleep a great deal. They don't eat very well. Just an altogether different neurologic hardwiring.

So, God-given brain programming, or neurochemistry – whatever you chose to think of it as – constitutes the wherewithal of psychologic temperament. We don't precisely know the true underlying mechanisms for this as yet, other than to say some persons possess a bigger bounty of available neurotransmitter substances – Serotonin, Norepinephrine, etc (i.e., the extroverts) – than is the case for introverts. And, no doubt other root cause specifics will be discovered in the future as to why we are all so different vis-à-vis our temperaments.

Sanguine

The first personality type I'll talk about is the Sanguine/Otter (*Sanguine* is LaHaye/Littauer-speak; *Otter* is Smalley-speak). You can easily recognize a Sanguine in a group setting. He is the person affectionately known as *The Life of the Party* (an obvious extrovert). These folks love to talk and visit. They live life enthusiastically, optimistically – full of energy. Young male Sanguines are frequently dubbed by teachers as *Class Clowns*.

And, of course, while Sanguines are busy having so much fun, other compartments of their lives become undisciplined, messy, with little or nothing ever finished! Other weaknesses include inconsistency, disorganization with schoolwork, along with absent-mindedness.

As a general rule, young Sanguines struggle mightily with boring/run-of-the-mill activities. Additionally, they regularly take the Olympic Gold for organizational problems, along with poor planning and lax impulse control. Thus, these kiddoes often place too little emphasis on studying for tests, getting school projects ready, etc.

As I say, Sanguines are outgoing, effervescent, cheerleader types. They love to entertain. They adore people, and they crave having fun. In fact, frivolity is what these individuals live for. "If it's not fun, don't bother me with it, O.K.? You want me to do something that's not enjoyable? Forget-about-it; I'm outta here..." So, the ever-present pursuit of fun is the chief priority of Sanguine life.

Moreover, Sanguines struggle mightily with what? What would you expect a person such as this to grapple with, avoiding at all costs? If your *final answer* was, "Being alone," you win a night out with Regis Philbin. Sanguines would sooner bite a pig than be by themselves.

What about self-discipline with the typical Sanguine? *Correct amundo.* Go a step further, and what are we talking about? Organizational skills? Righteo again. Typically, if you have a Sanguine youngster in the home, what happens to his homework papers? You saw him complete them; you checked them over. They made their way into the backpack. He gets on the bus...But something occurs to those homework papers after that, doesn't it? They're gone. Finito. Out-a-here. Mission Impossible. What happens to said homework papers? An excellent question. Prime fodder for Robert Stack's old *Unsolved Mysteries* TV show.

Bottom line: for a Sanguine to learn organization skills, someone has to teach these to him.

Choleric

The second temperament – also of the extroverted persuasion – is the Choleric/Lion. Choleric/Lions thrive on taking charge of the situation at hand. You find many a Choleric as CEOs of organizations and corporations. Folks with this temperament are natural born leaders. Determined. Self-sufficient. Immensely goal-oriented. Frequently a classic *Type A* (*ultra-driven*) personality type.

Because the Choleric is **so** achievement-oriented, she can get into trouble however by demanding too much from others. She can also impress as bossy and short-tempered.

A youngster possessing the Choleric bent is, hands-down, the most difficult temperament of child to raise – quite the challenge to parents. These youth typically display blue-ribbon irascibility and oppositional-ism – classic *strong-willed* children, to quote Dr. James Dobson (Dobson, 2004). They're mouthy, opinionated, and very stub-born (actually of the oh-my-goodness stubborn variety). If we say "black," they say "white." If we say "up," they say "down"…Ahhh!!!

In a nutshell, our mission as parents is to help Choleric youth successfully navigate childhood and adolescence – short of causing, among ourselves, acute renal failure.

Melancholy

The Melancholy/Beaver, an introverted temperament, is the consummate perfectionist – detailed, task-oriented, orderly, analytical, organized. This person is able to see what needs to be done, and **do** it – a real worker bee.

My son possesses a Melancholy component to his temperament. I can remember as early as age 4 with him, we for example would dust his room. In the process, a small ornament on top of his chest of drawers might be moved…ever so slightly – perhaps 3 inches to the left of its original position. Well, 2 hours later he would commonly come in and say, "Hey, that's not in the same place – what happened?" As I say, Melancholics are generally detail-oriented.

As the name suggests, however, Melancholics *can* be prone toward depression – as well as anxiety – off and on throughout their lives. Other weaknesses of this introverted temperament are hypersensitivity, moodiness, and compulsivity. These persons can also impress others as insecure and difficult to please. They may furthermore be perceived as something of a *loner*. At the very least, Melancholics need private-time.

Also on the downside, Melancholics tend to be a bit thin-skinned on occasion, hypersensitive, and – as stated above – predisposed to intermittent depression. That doesn't mean all Melancholics become depressed. Just something that has to be watched a bit – not to say it's necessarily going to happen.

Frequently, a Melancholy youngster is pretty adept in school; she wants to please the teacher. She wants to get papers turned in on time. There's good academic *effort* on her part.

Phlegmatic

The Phlegmatic/Golden Retriever is kindly and introverted. This person makes a great compadre, inasmuch as she is able to get along with most everybody, is friendly, a good listener, and very loyal. She also – generally speaking – is pleasant, cooperative, and patient. The Phlegmatic is the notoriously **easiest** temperament of child to raise!

On the other hand, as with the three other temperaments, there are weaknesses. Frequent adjectives along these lines for Phlegmatics consist of: timid, worrisome, indecisive. Moreover, this individual would rather take a bullet than enter into interpersonal conflict. The same goes for change. She also has a tendency to keep emotions close to the vest. Additionally, anger is a four-letter word. Phlegmatics are typically very uncomfortable with expressing hostility – at least outwardly. In fact, many are not even aware of when they *experience* anger!

Confessions of a Choleric/Melancholy

Generally, people can primarily be identified by two of the four temperaments. Just to let you know a little about me, I test out as a Choleric/Melancholy. So, I possess both extroverted as well as introverted tendencies. And, this admixture is common among people.

At any rate, I'm the kind of person who likes to get on the horse and ride. I tend to make decisions reasonably quickly, but my Melancholy side says that before I make a choice regarding something, I need to get all the information/data (all, as in *all*). I want to have my ducks in a row – "t"s crossed and "i"s dotted. Such a penchant for detail, as any law-abiding Sanguine will attest, drives them absolutely berserk.

Any self-respecting Sanguine would say: "Just *do* it! A plan?! A blue-print?! Hey, just ride! *Let it eat!*"

Well, as part Melancholy, that's not me. I have to first perform my own due diligence. Parenthetically, the primary Phlegmatic on the other hand can perform due diligence from now until the Lord returns – and **still** feel ill-at-ease with making a decision.

Temperamental Temperaments

One further note I need to make regarding temperaments is that there are two so-called *unnatural* combinations (Littauer, 1992). Such include: (1) the Sanguine/Melancholy; and (2) the Choleric/Phlegmatic.

It's intuitively obvious that the Sanguine/Melancholy make for strange bedfellows, given the gregarious nature of the one (Sanguine) – in contrast to the quiet/introspective quality of the other (Melancholy). Similarly, the Choleric's high *drive* and strong-willed decisiveness stand in stark contrast to the Phlegmatic's low-key, easy-going, laid-back manner.

If Marvin is identified as one of these *unnatural* combinations, I need to rule out (investigate) the following: (1) identity confusion re-sulting in a conscious or non-conscious personality *masking*; and/or (2) a Borderline Condition (Gray, 2004). The latter (and not at all to be confused with Borderline Personality Disorder) has to do with a certain sort of emotional disturbance – that, by the way, is usually easy to treat, provided we know it's present.

Maturity in Christ

Assuming our man, Marvin, comes to accept Christ as Lord and Savior, he can expect to see a gradual alteration vis-à-vis his personality temperament, over time. Let's say the youngster is a primary Sanguine/secondary Choleric. It's true; he will almost certainly never deviate from these. However, it's likely to be noticed by others that his *off-two* personality temperaments (in Marvin's case, the Melancholy/

Phlegmatic) will slowly – over the years – become more prominent. Yet, they will never completely overtake his primary Sanguine/secondary Choleric.

As I say – should Marvin mature in Christ – he will see his primary/secondary temperaments become less pronounced, while his *off-two* inborn personality styles gain more valence. This phenomenon – maturing in Christ – is precisely what Jesus talked about in the New Testament:

> *Therefore you are to be perfect, as your Heavenly*
> *Father is perfect.*   Matthew 5:48

My pastor and good friend, Dr. Bob Bender, at First Baptist Church of Black Forest, Colorado tells me that the original Greek word for "perfect" here is *telos*. Such is best translated as an amalgam of "perfect, mature, complete." In other words, a continual striving toward completion in Christ.

Another more contemporary translation presents Christ's words via Matthew 5:48 as:

> *In a word, what I'm saying is, grow up. You're*
> *Kingdom Subjects. Now live like it. Live out your*
> *God-created identity…*   (*The Message*)

At any rate, striving for *wholeness* or *perfection* is what Christ requires of us as Christians. And, I like to think of wholeness or perfection as joined at the hip with **balance** (see Chapter 7). So, as Believers – while we strive for wholeness and perfection – *balance* – in terms of our psychologic temperaments, also naturally follows along, doesn't it? Such is precisely why I say that Marvin's Littauer Personality Temperament profile will reflect a greater *balance* as he matures over the years, as a natural by-product of his Christian walk.

A Final Note

Each of the temperaments has strengths and weaknesses. When parents understand the neurologic hardwiring of their youth, they are then better equipped to discipline that child in the most effective/Godly manner. Caregivers can then tailor behavioral interventions to their own unique Marvin. Furthermore, by understanding *my* temperament as a parent, I can be aware of the ever-present danger of imposing my personality onto the child God has entrusted to me. As I say, this cognizance helps us parent Marvin more effectively.

Remember, one size doesn't fit all when it comes to discipline – or to most anything else in life, for that matter. The four human temperaments pretty much ensure it.

Chapter 7

Parenting Marvin

Guess what? We don't all parent the same way. Just as we weren't all parented the same way either. The manner in which you were disciplined – along with your own temperament – generally determines the particular style you use with your own kids.

For a young parent (or even a more experienced one), the way in which you raise your youngster may well (and usually does) grind up a degree of friction with your spouse. After all, your mate almost always: (1) possesses a different personality temperament from you; and (2) was brought up differently than you were. So, as a parent, we hopefully can be reasonable and flexible enough to work out with our spouse, over time, a Vulcan Mind-Meld style of disciplining Marvin.

At any rate, there generally are four basic styles for parenting Marvin, as depicted in Figure 7.1.

The Dominant Parent

Remember the 1979 movie, *The Great Santini* – starring Robert Duvall? Here, one of my all-time favorite actors plays an ex-fighter pilot who returns home from active duty, only to run his family as he did his former military subordinates. The chain of command, rigidity, and authoritarianism were rife within the household. Santini's 18 year-old son seemed to encounter the greatest difficulty with such a regimented domestic life. The other family members struggled also, however.

Dominant	Neglectful
⊵ Heavy on rules and discipline ⊵ Similar to running a military battalion	⊵ Few rules/discipline ⊵ The *Absent Parent* (e.g., *Father Starvation* dynamic)
Permissive	**Balanced**
⊵ Light on rules/discipline ⊵ Heavy on love/warmth (A lack of discipline as a child will frequently result in the youngster having problems as an adult, e.g., being fired from the first job, etc)	⊵ Proper rules/structure which are well understood by everyone ⊵ Heavy on love/warmth (When in doubt, adopt a bit more love/warmth than discipline)

Figure 7.1 The Four Basic Parenting Styles

As with Santini, some of us as parents are top-heavy on rules and rigidity. Write it down: if your child has thirty-eight different rules to abide by, and you are a rigid human being – brace for trouble. *Big* trouble. Your kids will likely rebel. Some will overtly rebel (getting into drugs/alcohol, becoming oppositional and/or aggressive, for example). Other youth will make your life miserable in a passive-aggressive manner. Stepped in what?! A *passive-aggressive* manner.

Passive-aggression simply refers to the act of indirectly displaying hostility. Examples? Sure. Here's a list of our culture's Passive-Aggression Hit Parade among youth: (1) making bad grades – kinda' sorta' on purpose; (2) procrastinating/lollygagging on home-work, chores, etc; (3) hanging out with ne'er-do-well peers; and (4) serving up the *All-American Silent Treatment*.

For **adults** in our culture, typical passive-aggression fare include: (1) procrastinating/lollygagging; (2) withholding intimacy toward one's spouse; (3) frequent physical/somatic ailments devoid of underlying organic causes (e.g., some types of headaches – see #2 above); and (4) the *All-American Silent Treatment*.

Ah, quite a bit of overlap between youth passive-aggression and adult passive-aggression. The main point here to remember though is that, similar to Santini's family, persons who feel overly controlled in a rigid manner by someone of higher authority will almost always rebel. Some will overtly kick and fume. Others will protest covertly – aka the above-mentioned passive-aggressive modus operandus (MO).

Bottom Line Number 1: I don't want to be a *Dominant* Parent.

The Neglectful Parent

These folks are all too common in our society today. Persons strung out on crack who nonetheless produce children. Individuals who constantly are absent from the home (e.g., a *Father/Mother Starvation* dynamic). If I'm frequently in *La-La Land* via the effects of cocaine, or if I'm never home for my youth, rules and discipline are going to be lacking. Worse yet, I'm not around to nurture my kids, or to teach them moral values.

As a pediatric neuropsychologist who has spent the last 12+ years working with neglected/abused children, I have seen first-hand the kind of *narcissistic injuries* that a lack of consistent parenting can produce (Gray, 2004). By narcissistic injuries, I mean: youngsters who have been maltreated, thus developing age-inappropriate self-centeredness as well as an almost total disdainment for rules. Any rules.

Bottom Line Number 2: I don't want to be a *Neglectful* Parent.

The Permissive Parent

When thinking about the *Permissive* Parent, I can't help but hearken back to my years working with troubled youth in psychiatric hospitals. As you can imagine, we quite often would have a World-class hellion teen admitted to the unit. Let's call him Adam. More often than not, Adam was regularly engaged in shoplifting, physical aggression toward Mom and Dad, taking drugs, flunking out of school, constant *profanitus vomitus*, etc, etc.

As staff persons, we would all brace for Adam's first day of admission to our unit. BATTEN DOWN THE HATCHES – ADAM WILL BE HERE TODAY AROUND 5 P.M.

Well, guess what? After 2 hours or so of initial posturing by Adam, what usually happened? He would calm down, start obeying our rules, and behave as a civilized human being. Hmm, this wasn't the feral child we were led to believe – raised by wolves, after all.

Turns out, I've seen a boatload of Adams admitted to psychiatric facilities, in Texas and Nebraska, over the years. (By the time I moved to Colorado in 1999, managed care had virtually gutted the nation of youth psychiatric units. But that's a soap box for another day.)

At any rate, the vast majority of Adams suddenly got much better, within a couple of hours after coming into us. So what's up with *that*?

Well, many Adams had been accustomed to no discipline and no rules at home. They virtually came and went as they pleased – despite hailing from loving families with well-meaning parents – good people. But, as a result of all the unstructured free-wheeling, Adam was immensely insecure.

Insecurity among young persons breeds acting-out.

So, upon coming into us, Adam now suddenly had rules, a schedule, supervision, discipline, and one–two–three–four walls. In short, he now possessed **structure** in his life. Adam's internal cesspool of insecurity had just been exponentially reduced. Thus, no need for so much malevolent posturing.

Now, I'm not saying a 2-week psychiatric admission was an *Adam panacea*, but it was a heck of a good start. As the young man was counseled and constantly held accountable for his behavior, we also worked with his parents, tweaking under the hood vis-à-vis setting up appropriate rules and discipline at home. So, if Adam's mom and dad **had** been among the *Permissive* persuasion, we worked to get that re-adjusted.

Parenthetically, I'm not suggesting that every youth who needs psychiatric hospitalization comes from *Permissive* primary caretakers. For many of the youth we saw, June and Ward Cleaver wouldn't have been enough. Even world-class Christian parents are usually no match for a youngster with, say, a neurochemical imbalance. But......

Bottom Line Number 3, I don't want to be a *Permissive* Parent.

The Balanced Parent

The longer I live (having turned 51 this year), the more impressed I am with the notion of *balance*.

In all things.

For all endeavors.

Personally, my own life is one never-ending quest for balance. If I partial out my personal existence into clumps, there are several. The same holds true for you, I suspect. There is the marriage clump. The parent clump. The church clump. The vocation clump. The recreation clump. We all possess most of these various clumps.

For me, anytime one clump becomes top-heavy, I have to re-titrate my clumps. "Wow, I spent two evenings last week doing the church clump. I need to bump up my marriage and parent clumps this week."

"Whoa, logged 55 hours on my vocation clump this past week; need to beef up my marriage, parent, and church clumps ASAP."

See, for me, achieving clump balance is an ongoing task of life. It's ever-present. Very same for how we parent. Check out again Figure 7.1. The Balanced Parent establishes a nice blend of clear rules and structure, along with a boat-load of love and warmth – laced with a healthy dose of anti-rigidity.

Sort of like a nutritious Tex-Mex Combo Plate. (I love oxymorons, by the way.) I've got of couple of cheese enchiladas, a beef taco, a half-dozen nachos, two chalupas, plus some rice and beans. Balanced – what any good Tex-Mex platter should be all about. Can you say Amen?

By the way, a Balanced Parent can overcome child-rearing mistakes – which we all make. Said another way, our offspring won't be psychologically blighted by our disciplinary faux pas – when such occur within the context of Balanced parenting.

Moreover, a Balanced Parent stands the very best chance of helping Marvin learn what it takes to do his best on the *job*.

Bottom Line Number 4: I do want to be a Balanced Parent.

And I'm hoping you do too.

Chapter 8

Marvin, The Dependent Underachiever

How many times have I heard the parent of a Dependent Under-achiever (DU) say, "As long as I *sit* with Marvin, he can do his homework. But, the moment I leave his side, everything goes south…"

Obviously, such is very unsettling to a parent. Why? Because there is the fear that Marvin will still require this same ilk of supervision well into his high school years – at the identical level of academic dependency. Moreover, in the back of our minds – whether we are fully aware of it or not – we worry that Marvin may never grow up (Whitley, 2001).

But, parents, take heart!

The very fact that you're reading this book indicates you are concerned about having to remain Marvin's second-skin, well into his teen years and possibly beyond. And because you **are** reading this book, we're not going to let that happen!

Just realize that the kind of dependency Marvin is experiencing – with you feeling as though you must eternally remain physically yoked to his side as the young man does his homework – is *n-o-r-m-a-l*! If it weren't, Marvin wouldn't be a DU, would he?

So, first simply make peace with yourself that this is the way DUs initially behave. You no doubt love Marvin very much. If you didn't, you wouldn't be here with me. And even though you may not (now, at least) believe in Marvin's ability to shed his DU yoke, be encouraged!

Remember: God is still in control, and He knows what He's doing (Holley, 2002).

Also please realize, we are motivated by people *believing* in us (Teaff, 1994). So, as parents, I need you to **act** as if you believe in Marvin – for now – until the rest of this book kicks in for you. Later on, you won't have to act anymore.

So, to get the situation turned around, read on.

Chapter 9

Marvin, The All-Powerful

As the parent of a DU, ever felt that the power level within your home is tilted in Marvin's favor? If so, don't feel like unto the Lone Stranger. As we discussed in the last chapter, pertaining to Marvin's seemingly suffocating academic dependency issues, his top-heavy power endowment (at *this* time, anyway) is normal.

DU kiddoes **do** have too much power.

But, there's no sense in you, Marvin's parent, beating yourself up about this. Just realize it's there, but that we *will* get the appropriate reins of power back where it belongs – to you. Remember, in dealing with DUs, patience and persistence are key (Whitley, 2001).

> *And let endurance have its perfect result, that you*
> *may be perfect and complete, lacking in nothing.*
>
> James 1:4

So first of all, what sort of power plays is occurring? Well, for one, there's what we talked about in the previous chapter – you having to sit on Marvin in order for him to do a scintilla of homework.

Then, there's that nagging dynamic of: "Gee, I'm a *lot* more worried about Marvin's grades than he is! And, if I'm more worried about grades than Marvin is, there's not a snowball's chance in Baghdad he'll learn to give excellent effort and do his best on the *job*."

Risk Factors for Too Much Power in Children

(1) **Giftedness:** These kiddoes often appear adult-like. They're very bright. And because of that, it's extremely easy for us parents to relate to them as we would other adults. The only missing ingredient here is what? Even though these youth are very intelligent, they still don't possess what? Maturity. Emotional maturity. So, it is often enticing for us to behave toward them as surrogate adults. As a result though, too much power is granted.

(2) **Birth Order:** Excessive power can be imbued to any of the following children: the eldest, the youngest, or an only.

(3) **Single Parenting:** Here, the oldest kiddo may become something of the confidant or partner to a single parent. We then may develop a *parentified* child – a youth who serves as a replacement for an adult's spouse. A divorce situation can obviously contribute to this.

(4) **Divorce:** If I'm divorced, and I have one or more children, what emotion is going to be very easy for me to experience? Right. Guilt. "If I'd just done something different, my spouse would still be around. Marvin would thus have his mother/father in his life. Now, he is suffering solely because of something I did or didn't do. And I feel guilty about this. As a result, what do I tend to do? Overindulge Marvin – not hold him accountable for his behavior."

(5) **Abuse and Neglect:** Young persons who experience either or both of these tend to develop traits linked to the *N-word* – Narcissism. Narcissistic kiddoes develop stubbornness, oppositionalism, and extreme selfishness – "The rules don't apply to me, thank you very much."

(6) **Early Sickness:** Any of us who has ever had a child suffer with a disease or developmental disability, knows what I'm talking about here. It's very easy in these instances to, again, over-indulge. We feel terrible that this happened to our youngster. What normal parent wouldn't? Often, a youth who suffers can be imbued with too much power. It's not something I as Marvin's parent set out to consciously do. It just happened.

*Adapted from Rimm, 1995.

Figure 9.1   Risk Factors for Too Much Power in Children

"If I don't hold my mouth just right, Marvin won't do any of his homework – even with me ever-lurking 6 inches away. And I don't dare discipline him for anything. If I do, he'll totally shut down on me academically. So, I have to let him get away with murder in the meantime."

Sound familiar? For any of us who has struggled with a DU, it does. But how did this all too-powerful-Marvin-madness get started in the beginning? Again, I look to the brilliant work of Dr. Sylvia Rimm (1995), the nation's pre-eminent expert in dealing with academic underachieving youth. She talks about common risk factors for how youngsters can get to be too powerful for their own britches in the first place. See Figure 9.1 above.

Bottom line, the very first step in dealing with an all-powerful Marvin is for me, his parent, to realize King Marvin is on the throne.

Keep reading to find out how I orchestrate a coup in order to restore myself to power.

Motivating Marvin

Part IV

Messing with Marvin

Chapter 10

Games Marvin Plays

What do I mean – a game? *Monopoly*? *Clue*? *Chutes 'N Ladders*? *Risk*?

No, I'm talking about a psychological game. Not a board game. Remember the old book that came out over 30 years ago by Dr. Eric Berne (Berne, 1969), *Games People Play*? This little paperback discusses many sorts of behavioral exchanges that occur between and among people. Most of these games possess covert pay-offs, outcomes we're not even usually aware of .

An example is *One-up-manship*. I recall several years ago overhearing a conversation between two people at my church.

> *Person #1*: Our family has really been struggling lately. My husband just found out he is laid off. Also, our 10 year-old recently was diagnosed with Asthma.

> *Person #2*: Oh, I'm so sorry to hear that! *My* husband hasn't had a job in over a **year**. Plus, our 12 year-old daughter saw a specialist on Friday because of all the stomach pain she's been having off and on for months. She was diagnosed with Cancer…

Besides the exchange of information, what just happened with the above conversation? You guessed it. Person #2 just *one-upped* Person #1.

These sorts of interchanges among people are common. And, frequently they're harmless. However, in *One-up-manship* the hidden pay-off is what? Perhaps a seeking out of sympathy from another person. Maybe a quest for power in a relationship ("You think you have it bad – what about **me**?!"). On and on we could go, in terms of what the emotional/behavioral pay-offs might be in a game of One-up-manship.

Another example. I have a cousin, who is now grown. For purposes of protecting the innocent, let's call her Jill. During fourth grade, Jill's claim to fame was the old *I'm Too Sick To Stay At School Today Game*. Thus, this little pixie was getting sick a lot that year.

Here's the way the cycle went.

Jill would first complain to the teacher, "I don't feel so good..."

"O.K. Jill. Let's have you go down to see the school nurse." So, she goes down to the nurse.

The nurse looks at Jill, checking her over. Finding no fever or AWOL body parts, the nurse hears from Jill that her stomach nevertheless still hurts.

So what does the nurse at that point do? Calls Mom.

Then what does Mom do? Comes and picks up Jill from school, taking her home.

Anyway, this became a cycle during much of Jill's fourth grade year. Broken-record city. After the sixth or seventh such incidence of the *I'm Too Sick To Stay At School Today Game*, it was discovered that Jill invariably had a math test on the days she was getting sick. And she was none too fond of math. Hence, what was the obvious pay-off? Missing the *$^&#%@ **math** test. Pretty obvious, no? Not exactly rocket science. But it was gameyness at its best.

My point? *Games* can occur almost continually within our families. And, in the case of our man, Marvin, games are usually of epidemic proportions. In fact, any good DU worth his salt is a Jedi Master at gameyness.

All right then. So how do we de-game Marvin? Well, it's a two step process.

Step 1: We first have to become aware that a game is occurring. In the example of Jill, it was well into the latter stages of the Spring semester before anyone determined that, in the words of good ole George Bush, Sr: "Math tests – *baaad.* The *I'm Too Sick To* Stay *At School Today Game – goood.*" (At least in the mind of Jill.)

Step 2: Once adult insight has been gained as to the underlying purpose of the game, at least one of the adult players must choose to step out of the game. In the case of Jill, who were the adult players? Right – Teacher, Nurse, Mom. In order to defeat the *I'm Too Sick To Stay At School Today Game*, either the teacher, nurse, or Mom has to make a conscious choice to remove herself from the game's merry-go-round. Better yet, all three can step off.

O.K. How could one of the adult players, on Jill's behalf, step off? One of them simply has to do something different. Hmm…

Let's look at some of the possibilities here. One option might be for the teacher to merely talk to Jill a bit prior to the math test, attempt to reassure her (after having orchestrated a program of, say, weekly after-school arithmetic tutoring) – before sending Jill down to the nurse.

The teacher of course can also indicate to the nurse that Jill's stomach pain coincides with days containing math tests.

Another tack would be for the nurse – rather than calling Mom – to allow Jill the chance to lie down for a while in the clinic office, sip some cold agua, and simply chill for 15 minutes or so. Then, send her back to class.

Yet another strategy would be for the teacher/nurse to speak with Mom on the phone and agree to a plan of attack for days in which Jill experiences test-day stomach pain. Then, rather than picking her up from school – in effect rescuing her from the blankety-blank math test, Mom decides she'll step off the merry-go-round and **not** take Jill out of school.

But the point is, at least one of the adult players has to step out of the game in order for matters to change.

Typically, who is the least likely participant to step out of the game? (If you said to yourself just now: "Jill", then have your spouse take you out to dinner somewhere other than Carl's Jr.)

Back to Marvin. As a skilled DU, what are some of the more common games we'll see from him? Correct – you're already ahead of me. MIA written assignments. Lollygagging during homework. Denials that he heard you say, "Marvin, be sure to ask Ms. Jones today about the upcoming history test." (The latter is known as *selective deafness*.)

Games Marvin plays...

Allowing Marvin to continue unabated in his gameyness – *Baaad*.

De-gaming Marvin – *Goood*.

Chapter 11

A Befrazzled Marvin

Soccer. Band. Tae-Kwan-Do. Football. Piano. Girl Scouts. Voice. T-ball. Soccer. Drama. Tennis. AWANAS. Tap-dancing. Equestrian Training. Art Class. Honors Society. Spanish Club. Wrestling. Flower Arrangement (advanced). Yearbook. Astronomy. Ceramics Anonymous. Rappelling Club. Madrigal Choir. Cross Country. Gymnastics. Debate Team. Lacrosse. Badminton Association. Swimming. Weightlifting. Figure Skating.

The variety of extracurricular activities our youth have to choose from these days is staggering.

Is all this *good* for kids? Yes and no, in my opinion.

On the pro side of the argument, our offspring in this day and age have more specialized activities available to them than ever before. As a result, youngsters who show a natural proclivity for music can really benefit – by way of self-esteem – from a 30-minute piano lesson once a week. Same is true for drama. Who knows, we may have a future Kevin Spacey on our hands.

On the con side, loading our kids up with too many after-school extracurriculars may **make** them spacey.

So, are we weighing down our youth with onerous dosages of after-school appointments as we seek to live life through them vicariously. If so, we're into Deep Voodoo (Perot, 1992).

How often have I heard parents say to me – upon my attempts to help their child out of the DU abyss – "Well, we can't exactly drop Wednesday afternoon macramé class, now can we?! So how is a *Motivation Plan* (see Chapter 33) with Marvin going to work?!"

That's just it. It won't work. This dog won't hunt.

After all, Marvin is a kiddo who needs to develop independent academic skills. So he can learn to get his homework done expeditiously. Thoroughly. See, we're talking about priorities here, aren't we? Is it, for example, preferable to, at least temporarily, suspend weekly Tumbling Class – in order to create a freer after-school routine for a DU?

Well, candidly, I don't know the answer to that.

But if you, as Christian parents, spend time in prayer – meditating via guidance of the Holy Spirit – you'll know.

Here's an even tougher one. Should I, as a Christian parent, quit (or at least cut back on) my job – relying upon my spouse as chief breadwinner – thereby creating more time to supervise/structure Marvin's academics?

Again, I don't know. Not my call. This is your call. But, as a Christian parent, if you bathe this decision in prayer, wise counsel, and scripture reflection, the Lord **will** speak. You'll know what if anything needs to be done differently. This is what we call discernment.

> *But if any of you lacks wisdom, let him ask of God, who gives to all persons generously and without reproach, and it will be given to him.* James 1:5

Heck of a deal, huh. God's Word says that to obtain wisdom, all we need do is **ask** for it! Doesn't take an MBA from Yale, a medical degree from Cornell, or Ph.D. from Stanford.

The Bible says simply *ask*.

At any rate, the answer to the question of priorities is – *no one size fits all.*

Generally however, I **can** tell you this – speaking as both a parent and deranged Christian Shrink: I see way too many youth in our society today over-extended. I call this EED (Excessive Extracurricular Disorder). Not only does such induce wanton befrazzlement in many kids, it also obstructs their capacity to academically *do their best* (there's that mantra again).

	Marvin's Weekly Extracurricular Schedule	
O	Monday	Thursday
	4:00 Soccer Practice	4:00 Spanish Club
	6:30 Science Group	6:45 Tennis Tournament
	Tuesday	Friday
O	4:45 Piano Lesson	7:00 Before school band
		practice
	7:30 Tennis Lesson	5:15 Chess Club
	Wednesday	Saturday
	4:00 Soccer Practice	11:00 Soccer Game
	5:00 Scout Meeting	12:30 Leave for Scout
O	7:00 Choir Rehearsal	Campout

Figure 11.1 Marvin's Weekly Schedule

Admittedly, I grew up in a simpler era. Yeah, we **did** have at the back of our minds – in the mid 60s – a concern. "What if today the Rooskies decide to launch the big one – smack-dab at Carswell Air Force Base (30 miles north of where I lived: 903 Forrest Avenue – Cleburne, Texas)?" So yes, there was this ever-present, if generally non-conscious, preoccupation with nuclear devastation.

On the other hand, we didn't have to concern ourselves with EED. For me personally though, there was the one exception – a 2-month stint of 6th grade ballroom dancing lessons, conducted by John and

Helen Butner down at the local Episcopal church. (Still not sure what sort of brief reactive psychosis emanated from my mother, Juanita – along with the moms of Brad Wooldridge and David LaPrade. But that's another story.)

No, generally speaking, below is my K through 12th grade schedule:

The Author's School-Day Schedule, K-12
Circa 1960s

7:00 a.m.	Get up, get dressed, eat breakfast
7:45 a.m.	Ride bike to Coleman Elementary/Cleburne Junior High; later drive a beat-up pea-green 1962 Volkswagon to Cleburne High School – *Home of the Fighting Yellow Jackets*
8:00 a.m.	Arrive at school
3:15 p.m.	Dismiss from school
3:30 p.m.	Arrive home
3:45 p.m.	Finish after-school snack
4:00 p.m.	Play sandlot tackle-football (no pads – we were idiots) at Swatzell's Lot on Prairie Avenue – with Dave Stricklin, Mike Pritchard, Burton Baker, Mike Jenkins, Curtis Pritchard, Mike Dohoney, Larry Kemp, Woody Kemp, Donny Rinehart, and Brad Wooldridge (we almost always had enough for at least 5 on 5)
5:30 p.m.	Home for supper
6:00 p.m.	Homework
8:00 p.m.	TV/Free-time
9:00 p.m.	Bedtime for Bonzo (a later lights-out during high school)

Figure 11.2 The Author's School Day Schedule

Thaz it!

So yes, I am somewhat biased against kids having five or six private/structured lessons/activities after school each week. But, that's just me. If you as a parent have a God-led peace about whatever after-school schedule your youngster follows, you need to honor that (or in Texan golfer lingo: *Let it eat!*).

I suppose my point is: most youngsters don't do too well with EED. It can cause befrazzlement, with no favors to their mental health.

And, it gets in the way of their *job*.

Chapter 12

Marvin, The Lifer

Remember those old gangster movies? The ones where the guy's in The Big House – for life? No real incentives to do much there. He guy can't get out on early parole because, well, he's a Lifer.

Doesn't really behoove him to become the very best license plate manufacturing *ar-teest* San Quentin has ever seen. No particular benefit in starting up a Tuesday Men's Bible study on Cell Block 10. Why? He's a Lifer. No matter what *good* he does, he's not going anywhere!

The very same dynamic exists with kids who have been over-grounded.

"I've taken away everything **possible** from Marvin. He can't go outside or see his neighborhood friends for the next 8 years. What else am I supposed to do to him?!"

Well, good question. Marvin has become a Lifer. Not at Leavenworth. At your home. He has no incentive to do better – schoolwise, via his oppositionalism, or at *anything* for that matter. He's a Lifer.

"Doesn't matter what my behavior is. I'm still grounded until age 34..."

What to do?

Well, for one, we as parents need to keep our groundings S&S (sharp and short). Yes, they should bear valence (sharp). But, they should also be durationally crisp (short) – so that Marvin can see light at the end of the tunnel.

S&S.

61

This is precisely why I like *daily* groundings.

"The bad news, Marvin: no TV, phone, or Nintendo for the rest of the afternoon and evening due to today's zero on your Language Arts paper. The good news: tomorrow's a brand new day!"

The Lifer Syndrome. "Not gonna do it..." (Bush, 1990).

Chapter 13

End-Runs and Marvin

DUs for whom a Motivation Plan (see Chapter 33) is set up will attempt all manner of end-runs. Make peace with it. These are done to avoid taking on more academic responsibility than they're accustomed to. Just human nature. "Hey, I'm used to my *parents* worrying about how I do in school – why should I take on the burden?! What, are you crazy?!"

As I tell parents, for me to **not** warn them about ERS (*End-Run Syndrome*) is tantamount to malpractice. So, expect matters to get worse – not better – over the first couple of weeks on a Motivation Plan (MP). This is classic ERS in action: kids doing virtually anything they can think of to defeat the MP. "If I can frustrate my parents on this enough – right off the bat – they'll cave and go back to worrying about school *for* me."

I recall early in my private practice, 20 years ago. I was making two big mistakes of which I wasn't aware. The foremost faux pas was attempting to do traditional counseling with DU kids. But wait! This is what we are all taught in graduate school, isn't it?! "Counseling cures all ills. Bring me your tired, your frail, your huddled masses yearning to breathe free..."

If we simply do counseling with them – because after all we were trained in counseling...so that we can do counseling...in order to do more counseling...As a result they *will* get better!

Although traditional talk-therapy with Marvins never worked for me, consider Dr. Michael Whitley, a Houston-based psychologist and author of *Bright Minds, Poor Grades* (2001). From having read his book, I am impressed with how he in fact does use counseling via DUs, apparently effecting good success.

Most especially I am impressed with Dr. Whitley's use of the Socratic method: repeatedly asking teen DUs seemingly ridiculous/overly detailed questions. Such is for purposes of allowing them to gain insight into their own identity issues related to "forgetting" assignments, constantly being bored in class, etc.

Another reason piquing my interest while reading Dr. Whitley's book was his reference to Columbo-like questioning, as a tack with adolescent DUs (Whitley, 2001).

"Hey, Marvin, you say you forgot to bring your science book home from school today? Well, you already know I'm a little dense. So how did that happen exactly? I mean, you earlier said the last thing your science teacher stated, right before the bell rang – the last period of the day – 'Students, don't forget to take your textbook home tonight to study for tomorrow's test.' I mean, to *forget* in this instance would mean that your memory is so bad there's something very wrong with your brain, as if you're brain damaged. And I know you're not brain damaged. So I'm having a little trouble with this thing here of forgetting. Help out an old ignorant shrink please…"

At any rate, I too have long used Detective Columbo's interviewing style. Colleagues of mine have more than once said, "There you go with the Columbo routine again…"

Perhaps Dr. Whitley and I were separated at birth.

Anyway, all that to say, from reading *Bright Minds, Poor Grades*, I now have amended my erstwhile concerted pooh-poohing of counseling with DU teens. While my own experience – for *me* – has born out that working with Marvin's **parents** bears much more fruit than does doing sit-down counseling with him (especially for DUs 12 and under), I now concede Dr. Whitley's mode of counseling with adolescents can be effective.

However, most mental health therapists attempting traditional counseling with DU youth don't appear to be doing anything remotely resembling Dr. Whitley's tack. Anyway, for clinicians – as well as any parents out there reading this who think that more of a counseling approach will help their own Marvin – read *Bright Minds, Poor Grades*.

All right. Back to the topic of me making mistakes early in my practice. My second industrial strength e-r-r-o-r – once I finally figured out that non-Whitley ilk traditional counseling is an abysmal waste of time and money with DUs – was: *failure to caveat*. What do I mean by this? Here it is: upon first getting a family set up on an MP, it's crucial to warn Marvin's parents of the inevitable ERS (End-Run Syndrome) that *will* take place. (Parents, if you are fortunate enough to have a DU youngster who doesn't move into ERS mode, simply: (1) praise God; (2) count your blessings; and (3) celebrate via the best Tex-Mex spread you can find – preferably at Joe T. Garcia's in Fort Worth, Texas.

If, on the other hand, you're like most of us – who do encounter the typical ERS child, secondary to establishing an MP – merely realize that Marvin won't take the MP lying down. Things *will* get worse for a couple of weeks before they get better.

Just expect it, and don't worry about it. Some of the more common shenanigans that Marvin throws at us are shown in Figure 13.1 below.

How best to reduce the wallop of ERS within the initial stages of an MP? First of all, sit down with Marvin and broach – head-on – the behaviors listed in Figure 13.1. Also be sure to *reassure* him as to the specific consequences of an ERS. (Usually, this will entail a grounding of one or all free-time activities *for that day only* – see Chapter 18).

"Oh, Marvin, what's that you say? Ms. Perkins didn't initial your assignment sheet for math today? Bummer. Well, we have the old bad news/good news scenario here. The bad news: we're grounded from TV and phone from now until bedtime. The good news: a fresh start begins tomorrow!"

Common End Run Scenarios of the *Rich and Famous* DU

(1) Forgetting to get assignment sheet/planner initialed by a teacher
(2) Leaving assignment sheet/planner at school
(3) Losing assignment sheet/planner
(4) Blaming the teacher for refusing or forgetting to initial assignment sheet/planner
(5) Blaming the parent for not asking to see assignment sheet/planner
(6) Sneak-thieves abscond assignment sheet/planner from student on way home from school

---

Figure 13.1   Common End-Run Scenarios

I suppose what I'm saying here is: don't get discouraged, parents, by DU end-runs. They happen.

Speaking again of the good Dr. Whitley, I also like what he has to say about an historical comparison related to disciplining Marvin: "...Like the founding fathers of our country, we can win the war for freedom after losing most of the battles along the way" (Whitley, 2001). How true! With DUs, it may seem as if we're beating our heads against the wall for several months or years – attempting to get their behavior turned around – only for them to finally *get it* in the end. Amen. Praise the Lord. Pass the biscuits!

Another aspect that greatly helps is a parent who's willing to be enthusiastic, despite all of Marvin's past defeats. Indeed, enthusiasm *is* contagious (Teaff, 1994). Moreover, we as moms and dads can exemplify the kind of servant leadership modeled for us so ably by Christ, as we work with Marvin. In this regard, I really like what Dr. Gene Wilkes (1998) has to say about this in his book, *Jesus on Leadership*. We humbly serve God. In all endeavors.

Yes, Marvin's end-runs **are** frustrating. But they don't have to be defeating.

Motivating Marvin

Part V

Managing Marvin

Chapter 14

Independent Homework

Marvin gives the distinct impression that he is a total invalid when it comes to getting his homework done independently. Such, of course, leads to what? Right – *Homework Helllllllllll.*

Well, in a sense, Marvin **is** pretty much helpless when it comes to independent homework. Virtually all DUs are not even close to being able to get daily homework finished by themselves – at least if we're expecting it to be done well. Any youth can recklessly race through an assignment, giving not the slightest inclination for conscientious effort.

Thus, DUs are dependent upon **you**, the parent, for homework completion – at least if such is to be half-way competent. Moreover, DUs are world-class clock-watchers. They can wait out the afternoon/ evening with the best of them. When asked what he has been doing for the past hour – with not a scintilla of work-product forthcoming – Marvin's classic response is…drum roll please…"*I* oh-oh" (translated: "I don't know").

O.K., then. What do we do to start turning this massive cruise ship around to a 180?

(1) Be positive (Peale, 1987; Rimm, 1995; Teaff, 1994). Have a good attitude. I know, I know. Marvin gives you nothing to be positive *about*. How can you sincerely be upbeat with him, when it comes to academics?

That's just it. You can't.

You have to be an actor! As the old saying goes: "Fake it till you *make* it!"

What? How do you fake it?

Well, remember, we first have to set appropriate academic expectations for Marvin (see Chapter 5). If we could simply snap our fingers and allow him to become an independent achiever (IA), we would.

And you wouldn't need this book.

You first have to realize that training Marvin to become an IA is going to take effort on your part as his parent.

It will furthermore take time.

Lastly, reaching IA status will require doing some things *differently* with Marvin. Again, that's what this book is all about – giving you, Marvin's parent, effective tools to pull off some alternative interventions with him. Interventions that work.

But, it all starts with you, adopting a positive attitude.

(2) Prepare for an initial struggle (Rimm, 1995). If we have a child who has been accustomed to an after-school schedule of running, jumping, and playing – before starting homework at 7:30 or 8:00 p.m. – he's going to become a bucking bronco, kicking and spitting – upon being asked to do something different.

To not warn you that Marvin will initially proceed into behavioral contortions rivaling those of Linda Blair in *The Exorcist* – once we set him up on an MP (see Chapter 33) – would, again, be tantamount to malpractice on my part.

I learned very early in private practice to really emphasize #2 to parents. And then **re-emphasize** it. During my initial tenure of working with youth, I found out how crucial it is to emotionally prep Moms and Dads for the early stages of getting a DU academically turned around.

It went something like this. As a novice, I and the parents would work out an airtight MP with Marvin. I would next tell them to *prepare for an initial struggle*. We would then go forth to work the MP. Invariably though, after no more than a week, the parents would call or come in, stating: "It's not working. The Motivation Plan. It's not **working**. Marvin is hitting, cursing, and fuming – worse than before! This is not working! I thought you said this was going to work! I want something that works!"

Thus, I quickly discovered that, as consultant/clinician, I had to emphasize and re-emphasize to parents: "Marvin is not going to take this lying down. In fact, he'll initially get worse, before he gets better. It's just human nature."

So again, don't worry about it.

Just expect it.

We'll deal with it together.

(3) Provide a new workstation. Said another way, perform the ceremonial purging of the entombed desk. This helps sets the stage for homework independence.

And we've all been there, haven't we? Marvin has a room. And we're certain that at one time there was a desk in the room.

Furthermore, Marvin had a bed there as well. We recall buying the bed. It was a double bed. With a blue comforter.

But after a period of time, what happens? The desk and bed become buried. Somewhere in that room, covered by clothes and debris, a desk and bed remain.

Reminds me of my old college roommate, Rick Long from Atlanta, Texas – home of the *Hittin' Hares*. Rick was the most ingenious person I've ever known in terms of an ability to utilize furniture as a clothes catcher. (By the way, the Rickster later became a successful company CFO, and is to this day.) I'm not saying anymore about Rick in this book due to the fact that he has more on me than I have on him. But again, I digress.

Anyway, the purged desk or table should ideally be in a separate room, away from family traffic. No siblings should be allowed to interrupt homework. Jam boxes, TVs and tambourines are off limits within the initial stages of establishing independence.

Now, what will Marvin invariably say about all this: "What?! I don't get my jam box, my TV – while doing homework? Well, *Jenny-yyyyy* has all these when *sheeeee* does *herrrr* homework!!! That's not *fairrrrr*!!!"

Our low-pitched/dull-roar verbal response? "Right. And what, Marvin, do you recall about the grades Jenny makes?"

"*I oh – oh*....Maybe.... straight A's?"

"That's right, Marvin. When your grades reflect the same kind of effort Jenny gives in school and on homework, you can have a jam box and TV, too, when *you* study – should you still want them. Right now, Jenny has proven she can study effectively with all that."

(4) Learn to differentiate between Marvin's lack of under-standing a particular concept, and simple academic dependency.

For example, how many of us have heard: "Mom, I don't under-stand this stuff!!" Well, does Marvin really not comprehend the con-cept? For example, take figuring out adjectives and adverbs. Does he honestly not grasp the difference between an adjective and an adverb? Or, is Marvin merely into his classic dependency mode, wherein the *M-word* (ma-ni-pu-la-tion) reigns supreme?

So, what do we do?

First, tell Marvin to figure out all he can on his own before coming to you for help (Rimm, 1995). His response will be, "I already *have*!" But at least you've fired the initial verbal salvo in communicating that you're now beginning to expect more effort out of him. And, as Martha Stewart would say, "That's a *good* thing."

Almost certainly though, Marvin will shoot back, "I just don't un-derstand this..."

"O.K. Good. Tell me what you *do* understand."

"I don't understand *any* of it!"

"O.K. I need you to go back to your book and figure out some-thing in there you *do* understand. Then come back to me."

After trying the lesson on his own without success, Marvin can then, and **only** then, come to you for an explanation. Make him try an example question in front of you. Then insist he go back to his room to finish the rest. Such is of course in contradistinction to what? Exactly. Spoon-feeding him the rest of the way.

And, by the way, within the early stages of developing independent homework, don't be shy about using pregnant pauses with Marvin. Take the time to wait out receiving a verbal response from him – even if it takes 5 or 10 minutes. Remember, what is Marvin thinking if he stays silent long enough? That you're going to do what? That's right. Rescue him with the answer. "Not gonna do it!" (Bush, 1990). He'll soon learn that stall tactics won't work on you anymore.

Moreover, a word of praise to your spouse on Marvin's new independence when you see something he does well – i.e., providing effort – is key. And stating it within his earshot (Referential Speaking – see Chapter 17) will, over time, prove invaluable (Rimm, 1995).

By the way, interested and positive father figures are extremely effective in communicating a serious message concerning school work to DU boys. Such is also very helpful with daughters.

Just for a chuckle, if we could wake up Marvin in the middle of the night, before his pre-frontal lobes kick in – prior to becoming fully conscious – what would he say to us? See Figure 14.1 below.

You and I both know that neither of us should hold our breath with regard to ever hearing any of Figure 14.1 from Marvin. He'd sooner be boiled in lighter fluid. However, if he could somehow become aware of his needs, while simultaneously eating crow, this would be his academic wish-list.

Said another way, most Marvins have not been inconvenienced enough.

Wish-List for Dependent Underachievers

(1) Help me, Mom, become a better problem-solver. Give the problem back to *me*. That is, ask me to think about it for 15-20 minutes before I can bug you again for assistance.

(2) Help me, Dad, be accountable for my *effort*.

(3) Withhold your praise from me, Mom, until I give *effort*.

(4) Let me have the responsibility for what I do, Dad – as opposed to you taking responsibility *for* me.

*Adapted from Rimm, 1995.

Figure 14.1   Wish-List for Dependent Underachievers

It also bears stating that we as parents have to learn to deal with a degree of ambiguity in the early stages of helping Marvin get turned around. This is what Cornale (1992) calls *Letting Go Of the Moment* – only to come back later with a consequence of some sort, after the youngster has shown zippo effort.

For example, following a horrible bout of Homework Hell prior to dinner – with Marvin failing to do his work or cooperate – Mom chooses to ceremoniously *let go of the moment*. As a result, she stops the prodding, instead allowing him to spend the rest of his afternoon in time-out, until Dad gets home. Neither the time-out (if carried out properly – see Chapter 19), or Dad getting home, will be pleasing to Marvin.

By the way, I'll be talking more, in Part VI, about helping Marvin increase his level of independence when it comes to getting after-school assignments completed.

Stay tuned!

Chapter 15

Self-Esteem

If you asked most parents, "Name the one thing you'd most like your kiddo to possess," what would their answer be? Right. Good self-esteem.

Unfortunately, pop psychology has done a poor job of communicating how healthy self-esteem is imbued to Marvin.

In fact, a solid self-concept is not really imbued at all. And therein lies much of the problem.

A healthy self-regard is not something to be given away, as though a grandfather's watch.

I do however realize that as Christians, God prizes us unconditionally. And, when we really come to internalize this truth, a low self-esteem can be mystically healed via the Holy Spirit.

But for most young persons, a solid self-concept, in the main, has to be earrrrrn-ed – E. F. Hutton-style. Simply **telling** Marvin how great, smart, fast, nimble, or talented he is only scratches the surface. In fact, *empty* praise (for example, verbally stroking a child as a stellar tennis player who in fact is only average) likely hurts more than helps.

The child, deep-down, knows he's not a great tennis player: "So why is Mom lying to me?"

Such simply erodes trust in a parent – "How can I fully rely on my mother, given that she lies to me?"

Rather, a healthy self-esteem is primarily earned by a person via blood, sweat, and tears. If, for instance, you examine your own life, how much of what you have – that you deeply value – came to you easily? Probably not much.

In my case, I derive a portion of self-esteem from my college degrees. Did these come without mass quantities of sacrifice and elbow grease? Nope.

I am also proud of my wife, Debbi. Did she come to me easily? Huh-uh. The Lord forced me to pursue her for several years before she would give me the proverbial time of day.

What about my modicum of musical ability. Easy? Niet. Innumerable years of involvement in choral groups, plus four years of professional voice lessons figure into the equation.

In short, we as humans have to work at what we're good at. Certainly there are exceptions. For example, a small percentage of the world's populace are natural virtuosos: the late Walter Payton in football, Luciano Pavorotti in vocal music, Albert Einstein in physics. But even these immense talents chose to apply mass quantities of concerted effort to their respective tradecrafts.

Likewise, the garden variety DU kid has to produce effort – *much* effort – in order to get untracked academically. And we as parents have to let Marvin struggle a bit on the journey. Bailing him out, by way of hovering, does more harm than good.

To be sure, however, I am not talking about thrusting the Alcoholics Anonymous' model upon Marvin: "They gotta hit rock-bottom before we can help 'em!" Although the AA 12-Step Program works great for alcoholics, it's generally an unmitigated disaster with DU youth.

On the other hand, we should provide structure and measured assistance to DUs. Some kids need a little. Some need more. But if we as parents take on the bulk of academic responsibility, Marvin suffers. He learns, "Mom is going to bail me out every time! Yessss!"

In truth, this type of youth internally whisper to themselves: "I think Mom is a lot more concerned about my grades than I am! Hot *dang*!"

Want Marvin to develop a healthier self-esteem vis-à-vis academics? Good. Let him give effort. Let him struggle a little bit. Not only will he: (1) become a better student; but (2) his self-concept will elevate as well.

It's a classic Kuppenheimer's *Two-Fer* Sale!

Chapter 16

The United Front

Yes, it *is* trite. The notion of parents becoming a United Front for Marvin.

However, this is crucial.

Children can become unbelievably oppositional if one adult allies with them, against the other parent (or a teacher). The end result? Marvin becomes more powerful than an adult (Rimm, 1995).

Not what we want.

So, when strategizing with your spouse, or the teacher, do it separate and apart from Marvin. Take him out of the loop. If he learns that Mom or Dad is all lathered up, one against the other – or versus the teacher, what's going to happen?

Exactly. Marvin will play that up for all it's worth.

Enough said.

Chapter 17

Referential Speaking

A word of praise to a spouse or other adult regarding Marvin, within his ear-shot, can do a world of good. This is called *Referential Speaking*, and is extremely powerful (Rimm, 1995). Such helps create motivation for what it is we are praising, and helps foster self-esteem as well.

Moreover, Referential Speaking provides added straw for a comfortable nest within the hacienda. A healthy emotional home environment is huge, when working with DUs or – for that matter – with young people learning to master the typically difficult art of writing (Feifer & De Fina, 2002).

Referential Speaking also dovetails nicely into the concept of coaching students – magnifying the positives, getting rid of as many negatives as possible (Teaff, 1994).

As Henry Ford once said, "If you think you can do it, you're right. If you think you can't do it, you're still right."

Same goes for our attitude toward Marvin.

Chapter 18

The Art of Grounding

Grounding has been defined as "the restriction of a youth's freedom, for a specific time period, or until certain conditions are satisfied" (Kaye, 1994).

Most of us as kids were grounded from time to time while growing up. During my early school years at Coleman Elementary – home of the Colts – in small town Texas, my friend, Jon Moser, seemed to be perpetually grounded. In fact, I believe Jon may to this day possess a listing in the *Guinness Book* for "Most Consecutive Weeks Grounded By An Obstreperous 10 year-old Male 4th Grader."

Anyway, grounding – similar to time-out (see Chapter 19) – is highly dependent upon technique. The error most of us make with this form of discipline is grounding Marvin for *too long*.

Grounding should occur, generally speaking, over 1 to 3 days at *most*.

Usually, no more than a single day.

Thus, when we ground Marvin (say, from TV or *Nintendo*) for 8 weeks at a time, we've already fumbled the snap from center. First of all, it's the rare parent indeed who can successfully enforce such a long grounding as this. Kids can almost always wear us down over several days' duration.

Moreover, mega-groundings merely set a kiddo up for the dreaded Lifer Syndrome (see Chapter 12). So, no matter how well Marvin starts behaving, it becomes moot – once he has initially been grounded – for weeks at a time. Marvin in his own eyes has already been jailed for all of time and eternity.

"I'm already grounded for 8 weeks; therefore, I have *nein/zippo/ nada* incentive to do any better – I'm a Lifer."

Much more effective is to restrict Marvin from whatever rings his recreational chimes (e.g., TV, telephone, *GameCube*, outside free-time, the car keys, etc) for a day. Such then allows us to repeat our old mantra, "Marvin, I have bad news and good news. The bad news: because of your MIA homework paper in Math that I found out about this afternoon, you're grounded from TV, computer games, and outside play until bedtime. The good news is: tomorrow's a clean slate!"

Should Marvin become unglued, the first course of action is to leave his presence. Lock yourself away in a room for a half-hour if you have to. Remember, often times anger on the part of a youngster is an attempt to punish you enough such that you refrain from future acts of discipline.

Regardless, by shortening our grounding durations, we avoid the Lifer mentality coming into play. And, in so doing, Marvin's already depleted level of motivation doesn't simply get worse.

Chapter 19

Time-Out

I think time-out has received a bad rap. Often soundly *pooh-poohed* by parents and professionals alike, this procedure is frequently misunderstood. It's been my experience that time-out can be **extremely** effective with many youngsters – if administered correctly. On the other hand, an improper implementation of time-out is usually a bust.

Worse yet, bad time-out technique frequently makes a child's behavior worse – not better. Ouch.

Time-out should occur only for predetermined offenses which have been explained to Marvin in advance. Immediately following a transgression, he should be directed to the time-out locale – calmly and with minimal verbiage – devoid of shouting or teeth-gnashing by us. If the time requirement is 10 minutes, then the clock starts as soon as he is on location and quiet.

Once time-out has been served, no further discussion, haranguing, de-briefing or explaining should occur afterward by us.

After a few trips to time-out, a warning is frequently all that's needed to curb Marvin's oppositionalism. Make sure not to deliver more than one verbal warning. Then, follow through with the time-out if his behavior doesn't stop.

An important side-bar. Time-outs for Marvin should *not* take place in his own room wherein favorite games and toys reside. Such becomes tantamount to rewarding rotten behavior. Rather, this form of discipline should be served up within a sterile setting – the blandest of the bland – where Marvin cannot *see* what is going on within the rest of the family.

Parents seeking additional information on this technique should consult Dr. Sylvia Rimm's "Recipe for Successful Time-Outs" from her book, *Why Bright Kids Get Poor Grades* (1995). Dr. Rimm includes some of the common mistakes we as parents frequently make, automatically ensuring time-out failure. See Figure 19.1 below.

Mistakes in Using Time-Outs

- When Marvin goes to time-out, he often slams the door. Parents respond by telling him **not** to slam the door. Marvin thus realizes he has power over his parents, and continues to slam the door!

- Sometimes, when Marvin calls out and asks how much time he has left, parents make the mistake of talking to or actually arguing with him. *Any conversation during time-out cancels the beneficial effects.*

- Some parents are hesitant about locking the door and will hold it closed, or not even close it at all. If the parent holds the door, Marvin knows the parent is holding it, and thus – *wha-la* – a power struggle ensues. If the door is not closed at all, Marvin may walk in and out, proving that the parent is not, after all, in control.

- Sometimes after Marvin has thrown objects around the time-out room, parents insist he go back to pick up what has been tossed about. Another power struggle ensues, in which case Marvin again takes charge of the parent – via another argument. Best to set up a time-out room which is fairly impervious to mayhem and destruction, by removing anything of value from it.
- Sometimes parents use a time-out only after they've yelled, screamed, or lost their temper. That's too late. Time-out has to be executed calmly, showing that the parent – not Marvin – is in charge.

Adapted from: Rimm, Sylvia. *Why Bright Kids Get Poor Grades* (1995).

Figure 19.1 Mistakes in Using Time-Outs

Time-Out for Teens

Some youth are too big/old for the traditional time-out technique. But, there **is** an adaptation (Rimm, 1995). Upon commencement of arguing or ranting by a teen, the parent can time *herself* out behind the locked door of choice (preferably while having a back-up family member such as a spouse at home). Thus, Mom (in this example) is spared from Marvin chasing her around the house with an endless barrage of arguments/excuses/pleadings. She then takes a hot bath or reads a magazine.

Often, Marvin will target one parent over the other to more thoroughly harass. Thus, allowing the victimized parent to go into time-out can be very effective. This shuts off the teen's reward source. One caveat: using Time-out for Teens will probably result in a temporary escalation of behavior. So, just be prepared to weather this, without overreacting or gnashing of teeth.

The author demonstrating to students that one can never have too many fall-back vocational options.

Following an admonition to students on the merits of avoiding MIA
homework papers, retribution abounds from three lovely
co-eds (left to right) – Stephany, Kelsey, and Bryana – painfully
reminding the author of countless female rejections from his college days.

Lecturing biology lab students about the need for stellar study skills
can have its drawbacks.

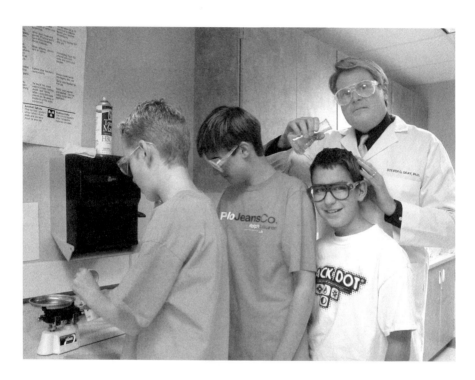

Pay-back is sweet.

A tireless study-animal, the author serves as exemplary role model
to adoring students.

The author receives a well justified scolding from principal, Dr. Barb
Masciarelli. Déjà vu all over again.

Chapter 20

Toxic Verbal Gameyness

Tired of all the mouthiness and debating that goes on with Marvin? It *is* possible to significantly reduce the amount of verbiage used with him – diffusing what I call TVG – *Toxic Verbal Gameyness* (Gray, 1999). As we know, many a Choleric/Narcissistic youngster is all too quick to verbally challenge authority figures.

But, it takes two to argue, and there's nobody holding a gun to our heads – shouting, "Debate!"

Not only is TVG tremendously draining for us as parents, but such also constitutes a subtle means of enhancing Marvin's inappropriate power base within the home.

One mistake we make is to exchange a great deal of stale information with Marvin. Rather, simply allow tangible consequences to impact him – pursuant to his failure to provide effort, or from his spewage of verbal vitriol at us. Instead, we fall into the siren-song allure of orally re-explaining why Marvin's behavior is *nicht so gut*. He **knows** his actions are tacky. He **knows** the rules.

There's simply no need to regurgitate them over and over.

Such is not only a waste of time; it's actually counterproductive. Marvin is merely empowered. In a way we don't want. Unfortunately, American culture over-values talking, explaining, pontificating, debating, *ad infinitum, ad nauseam* to our children as we lovingly mete out discipline to them. This tack is a quick road to oblivion. Moreover, with TVG we lose ground with Marvin, in terms of attempting to reduce his bloated power base.

If Marvin is constantly arguing within the home, it means he has established *gamesmanship* (see Chapter 10). Hence, it's incumbent upon us to forego Adkins or South Beach, and go on the Rocky Mountain Debate Diet. *Marvin* can certainly rant and rave...to his little heart's content. However, as I say, it takes at least two persons to argue.

Thus, we have to gently, yet firmly, lay down the law to Marvin that from now on debate club has permanently been disbanded.

The real art form of course with this approach is our ability to communicate the anti-debate message in a matter-of-fact/low-key manner – adding in that all-important dash of subtle jocularity, as in: "Oh, Marvin, remember? I was kicked off debate team in high school. I'm really lousy at it...Sorry!"

So, once again, we look to the inimitable George Bush, Sr. "TVG – baaaad. No debate club – gooood."

Chapter 21

The Anti-Arguing Technique

As a follow-up to the previous chapter, there are some practical tips that work in short-circuiting the arguing ritual Marvin brings at us.

Step 1: When Marvin The Arguer comes at you: remind yourself not to say yes or no immediately. Instead, after he has made a request, ask for his reasons. In asking for such, the young man can never accuse you of not listening (Rimm, 1995).

Step 2: After hearing Marvin's reasons, say: "Let me think about it. I'll get back to you..." For a small request, take a few minutes, or wait until after dinner before giving your reply. For larger favors, delay your response until tomorrow or the weekend (Rimm, 1995).

There are three marvelous benefits to Step 2. First, it allows you to be rational. Second, it teaches Marvin the virtue of patience. Many youngsters demand instant gratification; so forbearance is a good quality for them to learn (Rimm, 1995).

Third, given that Marvin knows you have yet to respond with either a yes **or** a no, he realizes that being *good* increases the likelihood of receiving a favorable answer from you later on.

Step 3: Think about Marvin's request and his reasons. Don't be adversely biased by your feelings or pushiness on his part. If the answer is yes, smile and say so. Be upbeat. Choleric/Narcissistic youngsters rarely see adults smile. If the decision is a compromise, explain such enthusiastically. If your answer is no – and parents *do* have the right and obligation to say *nein* – even if only because you are too tired to drive Marvin someplace – then say so calmly and firmly (Rimm, 1995).

It's fine to include your reasoning as part of the refusal. Rimm (1995) recommends keeping to your original decision at a rate of approximately 90%. Feel free though to rethink your choice 10% or so of the time, for flexibility's sake. Rigidity rarely has a place in child-rearing. But, either way, don't engage in further discussion.

And don't let Marvin make you feel guilty (guilt-jerking). Choleric/Narcissistic youth are of Olympic caliber at this. Such is a prime form of the M-word (manipulation). "If I can get Mom to feel guilty enough, she'll *cave...*" Don't get sucked into the abyss of being manipulated.

So, to re-cap:

Anti-Arguing Technique

Step 1: Hear Marvin's request – listen to his reasons.

Step 2: Think about it all carefully.

Step 3: Then – after a time – give your answer, as well as your rationale.

The discussion is now **OVER**.

Adapted from: Rimm, Sylvia. *Why Bright Kids Get Poor Grades* (1995).

Figure 21.1 Anti-Arguing Technique

Should Marvin continue his verbal barrage, and is below age 10 and not too big, send his little bottom to time-out (see Chapter 19). Or, withhold a privilege (see Chapter 18).

Eventually, Marvin will come to learn that you have the prerogative of saying no.

Chapter 22

Navy Seal Parenting

I have a great deal of admiration for the U.S. Navy Seals. In fact, I feel the same way about all our military – be they regular, or special forces. In fact, we can all learn much from our nation's soldiers and sailors – especially the Navy Seals.

What do I mean? Well, first of all, a Navy Seal team is small – usually only six people. These highly trained operatives are *not* heavily armed, relatively speaking. They do, on the other hand, thrive upon speed and stealth.

What is the last thing a Navy Seal wants to attract? You got it. Attention. Get in – accomplish the mission quickly, and get out.

Get **in** and get **out**.

As parents, it's a similar dynamic. When disciplining Marvin – in situations wherein he's clearly broken a role – we need to *get in and get out.*

Consider the example of mouthing off to Mom – say, in response to breaking a well-established rule that Marvin's handwriting must be legible. Tell me which of the two scenarios below most resembles a Navy Seal Parent.

Scenario #1

Marvin: "Mom, you're a stupid idiot, and there's no way in this lifetime I'm going to copy that paragraph over again!"

Mom: "Marvin, how many times have I told you – your writing *has* to be legible?"

Marvin: "I don't care. I'm not doing it over."

Mom: "Marvin, you know your writing has to be readable. If you don't do it over *right now*, you'll be in big trouble!!!"

Marvin: (Slamming a book down on his desk) "Oh, yeah?! Make me, you old goat!"

Mom: "Marvin, I've had just about *enough* of your mouth. If you don't stop talking to me that way, and copy your paragraph over again right now, you're going to be grounded – big time!"

Marvin: "Go suck a dill pickle!"

Scenario #2

Marvin: "Mom, you're a stupid idiot, and there's no way in this lifetime I'm going to copy that paragraph over again!"

Mom: "Oh, I *see*…Bummer (voice becoming lower in decibels). Looks like no privileges (Marvin/Mom wind-talking – translated: no TV/computer/*Nintendo*/outside play) for the rest of the day."

Marvin: "Go suck a dill pickle!"

Mom: (Slight yawn, calmly implements grounding.)

O.K. If you guessed Scenario #2 as the Navy Seal Parent, go to the head of the class. What did Marvin's Mom do in Scenario #2? Right. She refused to let him verbally bait her. She *got in and got out.* Then, Mom carried out the grounding.

Yes, this will take some effort. But aren't we asking *Marvin* to jack-up **his** effort level also?

Learn to become a Navy Seal Parent.

Chapter 23

Audio Therapy

Another means of countering oppositionalism from Marvin is Audio Therapy (Gray, 2000). Such involves utilization of a small, inexpensive micro-cassette recorder to capture episodes of verbal sassing.

Audio Therapy can also be effective with a tantruming Marvin.

First, have your cassette player handy at home. As soon as the rampage begins, commence recording. Such can be immediately, or later on, played back for Marvin – as well as other family members to hear.

Again, it's crucial that Audio Therapy be done in a light/tongue-in-cheek fashion. "Whoa! Let's hear that sound-bite *again*, Marvin!" Then, do an instant replay.

Mixing low-key humor into our disciplinary forays is extremely effective. With teaching **and** coaching, the value of jocularity is huge (Teaff, 1994). Humor also releases endorphins in the brain which make us feel better.

And with Marvin, I think you'd agree, we *need* to feel better!

Chapter 24

VideoCam Therapy

Similar to Audio Therapy, VideoCam Therapy (Gray, 2000) targets Marvin's ballistic episodes.

This strategy begins with informing the young man that we will, from now on, be needing to film some of his tantrums for use in the upcoming horror comedy: *Frankenstein Meets Saddam Hussein,* by Ron Howard – starring Gene Hackman and Clint Eastwood – with a brief cameo appearance by Stone Cold Steve Austin.

Then, keep your trusty camcorder at the ready, in order to tape a piece of the next Marvin-induced mayhem.

Once a video clip is made, the excerpt can later on – at a parent's convenience – be watched, while concurrently providing a John Madden running commentary via what Marvin is doing *on* the tape. "Wow! Get a load of those lungs! What volume! You just can't coach that sorta thing, Al – some things are just God-given…"

Marvin should be home during the time (or times) of viewing, but not coerced into watching. However, most kiddoes' curiosity snares them, as to how they look and sound on tape.

Marvin has likely never before considered how his tantrums actually play out in raw realism. Thus, he receives a therapeutic jolt by seeing his own ballistics in resplendent technicolor.

Chapter 25

Bland Sandwich Therapy

Another approach with Marvin is Bland Sandwich Therapy (Gray and Blue, 1999). Here, the young man is required – on days of restricted privileges – to eat a sandwich brought from home, as opposed to choosing an item from the menu, should the family be dining out at a fast-food joint (aka *rapid food emporium*, in the words of the inimitable Fort Worth, Texas psychiatrist – Dr. Ed Furber). We can also use Bland Sandwich while allowing other family members the luxury of carry-out from the local pizza parlor.

A favorite Bland Blue Plate Special of mine is a succulent slice of tomato, iceberg lettuce, along with a dab of mustard or mayo on Wonder Bread. Conversely, the traditional peanut butter and jelly will do equally as well, thank you very much. Just as long as it's bland, yet nutritious.

I recall a Marvin I worked with a few years ago. In Texas at least, there are Pancho's Mexican restaurants. At Pancho's, it's an all-you-can-eat extravaganza. First, go through the serving line. Then, once you're seated, should you desire seconds (which Marvin invariably did), merely raise the small Mexican flag adorning each table.

Well, Marvin on one occasion had failed to bring home his assignment sheet on a Friday afternoon. The family had planned a trip to Pancho's that night. Marvin got to go; however, he was on Bland Sandwich. While his siblings enjoyed the incredible sense of power that comes from raising the Mexican flag (which in essence commands an adult to bring them more food), Marvin was stuck with an appetizing mayonnaise sandwich.

Yum.

Marvin never again forgot to bring home his assignment sheet.

Chapter 26

Cell Phone Therapy

This technique can work within many different venues. It not only can be used within the school setting – but also church, club meetings, the neighbor's house, or any other situation wherein Marvin's behavior needs some carburetor tweaking.

For Cell Phone Therapy, the instant Marvin acts up in class, fails to turn in an assignment, or otherwise displays inappropriate behavior, he is directed into the hallway to dial up Mom or Dad on a *mo*-bile phone. He must then explain to you exactly what transpired – and why (Blue, 2000). Cell Phone Therapy obviously requires cooperation of the teacher or another adult.

The immediacy of this intervention, coupled with the sobering effects of having Marvin speak directly to you, his parent, while at school or wherever – can be powerful. At the same time, he also is singled out among his peers.

As such, Cell Phone Therapy serves up another potentially effective instrument in our tool bag for dealing with irresponsible behavior away from home.

Chapter 27

Back to School Therapy

Part of Marvin's academic problems rotate around the failure to hand in papers we know he's done. Are you as his parent, then, interested in a way to nuke this broken-record piece of nonsense?

Well, there is a way.

As with Cell Phone Therapy, discussed in the previous chapter, getting Marvin's attention in this regard requires some prior preparation on your part (talking to the principal and teacher(s) in advance) – as well as a bit of time out of your life.

What I'm talking about here is *Take Your Parent To School Day* (most school personnel **love** parent involvement with academic underachievers).

It's truly amazing how responsible Marvin can become when you decide that he needs a chaperone in the classroom (Dobson, 2004).

For this technique, after obtaining prior approval from the school, we accompany Marvin to each of his classes, sitting quietly in the back of the room. Don't say a word to him the entire period, or day.

Just being there is sufficient.

Follow Marvin from class to class, lagging behind him a few feet during passing periods. If he is younger and in a single classroom, simply camp out in one spot at the back.

Going to school with Marvin communicates to him that you are serious about doing what you can to help him *remember* to be academically responsible.

Back To School Therapy is one of the most effective means of one-trial learning for a DU that I have found.

Chapter 28

Electroencephalograph Neurofeedback

A promising collateral intervention for DU youth is EEG Neurofeedback (NFB). Such is showing *very* encouraging results for ADHD, LDs, along with mood/anxiety disorders. In addition, EEG NFB aids sleep patterns, various somatic symptoms, conduct problems, as well as drug/alcohol addictions (Amen, 1998).

In short, EEG NFB enables the brain to retrain itself via strengthening existing neurobiologic pathways, plus develops new pathways. This intervention is thought to be analogous to physical exercise. Research indicates that as the innumerable loops within the cortex and sub-cortex are modified (i.e., strengthened or redirected) by EEG NFB, such ensures greater academic learning, motivation, and an improvement in neurologic-based disorders (Lubar, 1999).

The first pioneer of EEG NFB was Dr. Barry Sterman (1974), via his seminal work in modifying seizure activity. For the last 30 years, EEG NFB research has demonstrated its role in the treatment of varying behavioral/emotional disorders (Amen, 2003).

Safety and efficacy are two huge pluses for EEG NFB. In essence, this treatment modality is akin to performing gradual/non-invasive brain surgery, without risk of permanent side-effects, when conducted by a well-trained clinician.

As more research is completed, EEG NFB may consistently produce better results than current psychopharmacologic treatment, with various and sundry disorders.

For Marvin, EEG NFB is another tool which can strip away complicating *chaff* – in terms of ADHD, LD, anxiety disorder – not to mention an increase in pre-frontal lobe motivation for kiddoes otherwise lackadaisical regarding doing well in school.

Although cranial training sites may vary a great deal according to the particular youth, I have found that many Marvins do well on an initial regimen of C3-C4 for an initial five sessions, followed by C3 alone (5 more sessions), and finally C3-FP1. C3-C4 are cranial sites situated over the central portions of the left and right hemisphere (approximately 3 inches directly above the tip of each ear). FP1 corresponds to the left prefrontal region (left forehead) of the brain.

Further information regarding EEG NFB technology can be found at www.eegspectrum.com.

Chapter 29

Psychotropic Medications: God-sent or Satan's Handiwork?

I won't keep you in suspense with this one. I strongly believe God has provided psychotropic medications for use in helping kids. It's the old notion of *All Knowledge is God's Knowledge*, and *All Healing Comes from God*. Having said that, do medicines with young persons sometimes get misused? Absolutely. No doubt.

But does this mean we should spit in God's face vis-à-vis a technology He has given us to relieve, say, a biochemical depression Marvin may be experiencing? The answer is yes if we believe Insulin should be withheld from a diabetic child.

My approach with parents? I see my job as laying out the various options – in terms of a possible medication for Marvin (along with behavioral and academic strategies) – based upon an initial/thorough NP evaluation (see Chapter 2).

On the issue of medications, I've found that parents generally rest within one of three groups: (1) those who are anti-meds; (2) those who are pro-meds; and (3) those who are ambivalent.

My solemn duty as a pediatric neuropsychologist is to: (1) hear where you as a parent are; and then (2) lay out the smorgasbord of psychotropic options, based upon Marvin's unique NP blue-print. I then thoroughly discuss the pros and cons of each specific medication with you – should such be indicated, once the results of Marvin's exam are back.

Thus, the use of pharmacology is not my decision. At all. Nor is it my right to make this call. It's your right – in cooperative synchrony with your physician. If I can emotionally support **you**, perform a comprehensive exam of Marvin, and then articulate what the options are – along with the associated pros and cons – then I have done my job.

Yes, I *do* cringe when a youth comes into me bathed in obvious polypharmacy. And yes, I *am* disgusted when medications are abused. But anything can be abused: religion, physical exercise, nutrition, and – medicines.

ADHD Medications

There are three different types of agents used to treat ADHD: psychostimulants, Beta-blockers, and anti-depressants. The one commonly prescribed, most familiar to everyone, is psychostimulants.

Psychostimulants

As the term implies, a psychostimulant increases CNS (Central Nervous System) activities: heart rate, blood pressure, respiration, etc. Overactive behavior from ADHD children is often thought to be a result of their own attempts to self-stimulate sleepy brain cells. At least, that's a theory. We for example find that when the pre-frontal lobes are neurochemically stabilized, an ADHD youngster often ceases *self-stim* behaviors – and consequently calms down!

Such is the case for the solely inattentive ADHD (ADD) child – who shows no component of hyperactivity. It's also assumed that there are too many sleepy pre-frontal lobe neurons. Thus, a psychostimulant may awaken these cells, allowing the ADHD youngster to lock-on phasers, Scotty – and pay attention in class.

Ritalin, Dexedrine, Dextrostat, Adderall, Concerta, Metadate, and Cylert are all psychostimulants. When a child begins on one of these, we always start with a low-dose. Such can gradually be increased, until the appropriate amount is reached. The old maxim of *start low and go slow* applies.

Regarding side-effects of these medications, the primary laundry list consists of: (1) appetite suppression; (2) insomnia; (3) headaches; and (4) irritability. Given that many youth brought in to me are *already* irritable, their parents kindly ask that we do our best to find a psychostimulant, at the proper dosage, which won't ratchet up irritability!

Side-effects may be short lived, lasting only the first couple of days as the child's body becomes accustomed to the medication. Or, side-effects can be persistent, in which case we then need to shift gears and try another psychostimulant option. Or lower the dosage.

Beta-blockers

A second class of agents used to treat ADHD is low-dose Beta-blockers. Researchers and clinicians fumbled upon the fact that low-dose Beta-blockers can be very effective with a subset of ADHD children. Beta-blockers' claims to fame are two-fold with regard to the ADHD population, reducing: (1) impulsivity; and (2) aggression. Therefore, if an ADHD child has either of these symptoms, there is a good chance that a Beta-blocker may be the best ADHD medication for him – at times in combination with a low-dose psychostimulant. Clonidine and Tenex are the two brand-name Beta-blockers most commonly seen.

Anti-depressants (Mood Elevators)

The last category of meds used to neutralize ADHD symptoms is an anti-depressant. SSRIs (Selective Serotonin Reuptake Inhibitors) is one of the newer subsets of anti-depressants. Here, I am speaking of: Prozac, Zoloft, Paxil, Celexa, and Luvox.

The first SSRI, Prozac, came out in 1988 – solely as a mood elevator for clinically depressed individuals. As is known, Prozac hasn't been without controversy. For example, some persons have claimed – unjustly in my opinion – that this agent causes suicidal behavior. On the other hand, I have seen first-hand this medication greatly help many depressed people. At any rate, suffice it to say, some people swear *by* it, some swear *at* it.

Serzone and Effexor are non-SSRI agents, but work in a similar manner. Another well-known anti-depressant is Wellbutrin, whose claim to fame – in addition to being a mood elevator – is to help people stop smoking. Moreover, among youth, Wellbutrin is considered by many to be the most effective anti-depressant in terms of helping neutralize ADHD symptoms.

Another recent psychotropic, marketed as an ADHD medication, is Strattera. Strattera is actually an SNRI (Selective Norepinephrine Reuptake Inhibitor). Hence, this is actually another form of anti-depressant. Strattera's popular appeal – to many parents' delight – is that it isn't a psychostimulant, and can be given once a day. The downside, thus far from my own observations of Strattera, is that it just doesn't seem to work that well for most ADHD youth. Admittedly, this is my personal perception of Strattera. Other parents and clinicians may well have a different take on it.

At any rate, the newer non-tricyclic anti-depressants (such as the SSRIs and related meds) work infinitely better than the old tricyclics (Tofranil, Elavil, Norpramin, etc) – and with many fewer side-effects. So now, non-tricyclic anti-depressants are the preferred first line of defense against depression. However, as I say, they are also frequently used to help neutralize ADHD symptoms as well.

So, what is the current mechanism as to how anti-depressants work in the brain? Basically, with psychotropic medications, all we have are theories, inasmuch as a functioning brain cannot actually be dissected. The closest we have in this regard is qEEG (quantitative EEG), PET (Photon Emission Tomography), or SPECT (Single Photon Emission Tomography). These technologies can detect the amount of either electrical activity – or blood-flow – to various regions of the brain. The variations in electricity or blood-glucose metabolism can often give clues as to how a specific area of Marvin's brain is functioning.

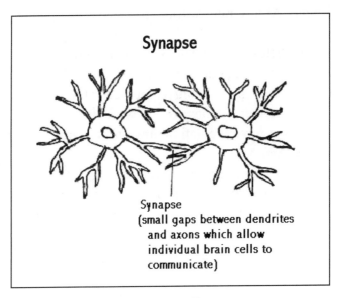

Synapse

Synapse
(small gaps between dendrites
and axons which allow
individual brain cells to
communicate)

Figure 29.1 Synapse

The space between individual brain cells (Figure 29.1) is called the synapse. In the synapses are substances (neurotransmitters) that allow cells to talk to one another, sending impulses from one cell to the next. You can think of neurotransmitters as the juice that allows brain cells to communicate. When someone is depressed or anxious, for example, the space between the cells becomes dry: sort of a micro-slice of Death Valley, California.

In the depressed youngster, as brain cells secrete various neurotransmitters, these same cells *take back* the neurotransmitter chemicals they have just released, thereby creating a deserty synapse – should they regobble too much neurotransmitter *juice*.

One of the neurotransmitters that is often greedily taken back in by the cells is Serotonin. Selective **Serotonin** Re-uptake Inhibitors, then, block the re-uptake – the process by which the cells take back the neurotransmitter juice they have just secreted. In this case, the particular juice is Serotonin. Thus, more Serotonin is left to remain within the synapses, where it can be put to good use.

Other juices enabling human brain cells to communicate are Norepinephrine and Dopamine, to name but a couple.

Personally, I like low-dose Paxil and Zoloft for kids who either need an anti-depressant as a mood elevator – or as an adjunct medication to neutralize ADHD symptoms. Again, this is my opinion. Other clinicians disagree, favoring different anti-depressants than Zoloft and Paxil. I can only speak from my own experience over the past 10 to 12 years of watching youth on these two agents (since the duo hit the market back in the early 1990s).

In terms of side-effects for low-dose SSRIs, typically the only thing I see is a little bit of cotton-mouth. It's possible for these medications to dry the mucous membranes within the upper respiratory tract. Once in a great while, I'll also see a youngster who becomes a bit agitated or irritable on a low-dose SSRI. But in my experience this is rare, provided the dosage is appropriate.

Among practically all anti-depressants we get a double benefit. What I mean is that these medicines are by definition mood elevators. But an additional bonus biggie via anti-depressants are anxiolytic (or in Plebian Latin – anti-anxiety) properties. So, if I have a youngster who is suffering from both depression **and** an anxiety component – which by the way is quite common – a low-dose anti-depressant will frequently help both.

Another use of SSRIs is for Borderline Condition of Childhood. This syndrome (not to be confused with Borderline Personality Disorder) is simply a state which can prompt a kiddo's perceptions of his world to be somewhat skewed. Or, this syndrome may usher in a subtle disturbance in his thought processing (Petti & Vela, 1990; Gray, 2004). Specifically, I have found that in about 50 to 70% of young persons age 10 and below who have been diagnosed with Borderline Condition of Childhood, a low-dose SSRI will send such into remission, within only a few weeks time, praise God!

Anxiolytics (Anti-anxiety Agents)

As stated above, the high-falutin' two-bit name for anti-anxiety medications is anxiolytic agents. Again, we have older, and newer types of anti-anxiety drugs. The old ones are: Valium (Vitamin V, as it has been monikered), Librium, Serax, Ativan, Xanax, etc. These medicines are all very effective in reducing anxiety. The down-side is their addictive nature. Hence, such generally are only used short-term, especially among young persons. Consequently, rarely are they given to children suffering with anxiety.

BuSpar, on the other hand, is one of the fairly newer anxiolytics on the market. Although technically an anti-depressant, this agent is almost exclusively categorized as an anxiolytic. BuSpar is nonaddictive. It has been out long enough for us to know that addiction to this med is impossible. Even if you worked at it.

Thus, BuSpar is quite benign, with a very low side-effect profile. Therefore, for a child struggling with acute anxiety, or a chronic/free-floating anxiety, BuSpar can be an excellent choice in my experience – owing to its gentle nature.

Neuroleptics/Anti-psychotics

The terms *neuroleptics* and *anti-psychotics* are synonymous. But anti-psychotic has such an emotional charge to it that I rarely refer to these agents in this manner. At any rate, both terms generally refer to the old-guard neuroleptics, including: Thorazine, Mellaril, Navane, Prolixin, etc.

Atypical Anti-psychotics/Neuroleptics

There's a new breed of neuroleptics in Dodge. And, they've proved to be a God-send for many youth. Actually, the more precise term for these is *atypical anti-psychotics* – consisting of Risperdal, Zyprexa, Seroquel, Clozaril, Geodon, etc.

Risperdal came out in the early 1990s. It's the one with which I have had the most success, partly due perhaps to its having been on the market longer than the others. Many young persons who need an atypical anti-psychotic medicine (for help with Borderline Condition of Childhood, for example) do very well with only a low-dosage, for a short time. Moreover, these agents are quite effective with Bipolar youth also.

One reason why atypical anti-psychotics are heralded by the medical community is their vastly reduced side-effect profile. Such is much lower than the older Thorazines, Mellarils, and Prolixins. With an atypical anti-psychotic, for example, the risk for Tardive Dyskinesia, a chronic motor tic disorder, is greatly reduced. No question though that the most vexing problem with *some* atypical anti-psychotics is weight gain. But, overall side-effects for atypical neuroleptics are vastly decreased, compared to the old-guard anti-psychotic agents.

Hypnotics (Soporifics)

The next category is hypnotics (soporific agents) – medicines that induce sleep, or help treat insomnia. I hardly ever see a child on a free-standing hypnotic. I do however frequently get a youth on Desyrel (generic: Trazodone) for insomnia. Insomnia is almost always a symptom of something else. So if a youngster *does* have trouble sleeping, I personally prefer to treat the underlying root cause of it. Common sources of childhood insomnia are: Post-traumatic Stress Disorder (PTSD), depression, and high doses of psychostimulants used to treat ADHD.

Anti-convulsants (Mood/Impulse Stabilizers)

The last category of psychotropics we'll look at is mood/impulse stabilizers. Here, we have: Tegretol, Neurontin, Depakote, Topamax, Lamictal, etc. These, in actuality, are anti-convulsant medications – originally designed for persons with epilepsy/seizure disorders. However, mood/impulse stabilizing properties also exist among anti-convulsants. Lithium isn't a true anti-convulsant, but *is* used for the same purpose as Tegretol, et al – as a mood stabilizer.

Lithium Carbonate (LiCo) is actually a salt found in the earth. Serendipity led to the discovery that many persons who suffer from biochemically-driven fluctuations of mood – or poor impulse control – stabilize with the use of Lithium.

Lithium was formerly the sole treatment of choice for what we used to call Manic-Depressive Illness – now termed Bipolar Disorder. Bipolar is the cycling of moods, wherein a person can go from the heights of grandeur and ecstasy, to the depths of Hell and depression – back up again, then down – similar to a yo-yo.

Childhood Bipolar Disorder (CBD) is however a different beast than the Bipolar Disorder that besets adults. CBD typically presents with chronic irritability, very rapid mood cycling, and ballistic episodes. Although Lithium has proven effective with a subset of youngsters who possess radical mood swings and/or persistent irritability, the above-mentioned anti-convulsants (Depakote, Tegretol, Lamictal, Topamax, Neurontin, etc) have almost exclusively taken over as mood/impulse stabilizing meds for kiddoes with CBD, not to mention Intermittent Explosive Disorder (IED).

By way of side-effects, Lithium can cause notable drowsiness, nausea, vomiting, fatigue, and increased thirst/urination. Similarly, adverse fall-out from anti-convulsants include: drowsiness, dizziness, confusion, and nausea. These side-effects usually occur within the initial treatment period – then subside – unless the dosage is simply too high.

Final Notes

Sometimes when a medication doesn't appear effective, it may not be the agent itself that's not working, but rather the dosage may merely be miscalculated. What if we knew, for example, via direct communiqué from the Lord Himself that, say, low-dose Wellbutrin (an antidepressant) was the medicine of choice for Marvin. But, we under-dose Marvin *on* the Wellbutrin? The result: we're making an e-r-r-o-r – falsely assuming the Wellbutrin itself is a flop. In reality, we just didn't have Marvin on quite enough Wellbutrin. So, care is needed with dosage titration.

Finally, using psychotropic medications with children is an intensely personal decision for you as a parent – something which can be quite scary.

But with certain mental health disorders among youth, a medication can make all the difference in the world. As earlier stated, I see my job as being the very best consultant I can be for both you and Marvin. Effectively communicating **all** the various options to help him – be it medications or no – is my privilege and responsibility. It's then up to you to pray over, seek out other wise counsel – allowing the Holy Spirit to guide – regarding the decisions that are best for Marvin.

As I frequently tell parents who graciously attend my seminars, it's not my right to force-feed broccoli down George Bush Sr.'s throat, if 'ole George can't tolerate broccoli.

The same holds for psychotropics.

Chapter 30

Tutoring

Unfortunately, one of the least effective strategies I've seen in attempting to get Marvin back to the Land of the Living is a Study Skills Program (SSP). These are generally very well-intentioned. However, in my experience, they don't work. Or more precisely, an SSP rarely works prior to successful implementation of an MP (see Chapter 33).

Simply stated, an SSP attempts to teach a youngster organizational/study skills. The problem: most SSPs don't do a very good job of initially instilling a *Motivation Factor* in kids. Rather, the garden variety SSPs I've seen merely seek to teach pre-adolescents and adolescents new behavior: for example, how to organize a school planner/notebook, how to take good notes in class, how to effectively study for tests, etc, etc.

The notion seems to be that if we merely instruct Marvin – much as we would an eager-beaver college student who simply never learned proper organizational skills or solid note-taking techniques in the first place back during their high school days, we can use the SSP to get an immature 13 year-old DU turned around.

It just rarely works.

Think about it for a moment. First off, the 13 year-old DU isn't motivated to be academically conscientious. Second of all, he almost certainly lacks the pre-frontal lobe maturity to in any way profit from having an adult instruct him, via the standard six to eight session SSP.

Rather, what Marvin needs is someone acting as prosthetic prefrontal lobes for him. And, I'm not talking about a hovering spoon-feeder parent. I'm talking about a person to effectively help keep him structured – holding him fully accountable for his academic *effort*.

And **he** must provide the effort.

We supply the structure, direction, and consequences. He provides the effort. In short, what Marvin first needs is a sound MP. Then perhaps, he can profit from an SSP.

Which brings me now to the question of a personal tutor. In short, once a solid MP is up and running, a good tutor can be worth his weight in gold.

But what kind of tutor are we talking about? An individual in private-practice such as a former professional school teacher? A national chain, a la a Sylvan Learning Center? I think both have value. The primary prerequisites for an effective tutor, in my view, are:

(1) Someone well versed in the subject matter confronting Marvin;

(2) A person with whom Marvin has rapport (which will help produce the all-important *MO Factor* on its own); and

(3) An individual who will allow Marvin to dig for answers (in contradistinction to a mano-a-mano lecturer for him).

I don't care how well an instructor knows his academic X's and O's, if a personal rapport is lacking between him and the student, kiss it good-bye. Same for a spoon-feeding tutor.

Again, never, never forget the *MO Factor*.

Do whatever it takes to ensure that appropriate consequences/rewards exist for Marvin – based upon the amount of effort (there's that word again). He must expend effort during each tutoring encounter. The professional – in the early going at least – should be rating (scale of 1 to 5, or 1 to 10 – whatever you choose) the effort level of Marvin. Every session. Then, appropriate consequences must result form the rating given by the tutor.

Another thing. As stated above, if you have a tutor that's doing all (or 90% of) the talking during a session with Marvin, find another person. Tutoring is interactive – a dialogue. It's not a monologue. So, parents, I encourage you to randomly monitor some of your youth's tutoring – sitting close by, within earshot – but out of view. You need to know what's going on in the sessions. Actually, you must know.

So, in summary, first do what it takes to establish the *MO Factor* (see Chapter 33). Then, by all means consider a first-class tutor to help with subject areas in which Marvin struggles. Not only will his academic skill levels increase, but a good tutor will help him develop something else very important: scholastic moxie. Scholastic moxie then leads to beefed-up self-esteem.

I am convinced that the best tutors are also mentors (see Chapter 31). Without high-powered role modeling, attaining academic moxie by Marvin is nearly impossible.

Chapter 31

Mentoring

As alluded to in the previous chapter, the best tutors are also mentors. Said another way, I rarely have seen an effective tutor who wasn't also a top-notch mentor.

I look back upon some of my own mentors. Take for example my adult cousin, Dr. Bill Whitehouse – the surgeon. Bill helped foster in me not only a desire for academic excellence but also an interest in the human body. How vividly I recall, as a middle schooler, him helping me organize various and sundry science fair projects centered on cardiology and gastroenterology. He also possessed artistic abilities. Bill was able to effectively draw sketches of internal anatomy for his patients. This was back in an era before so many professionally published charts and graphs existed on the human body. No problem for him though. Bill could sketch out anything you needed – an aorta, the duodenum, knee ligaments, or a femur.

In short, Bill mentored me by way of caring. Caring enough to allow a kid (me) to hang around his medical clinic, take him into the lab there, spend time with him. The message was clear. Bill loved and cared about me. Combined with my love and respect for him, the times with Bill provided a tremendous mentoring relationship for a strong-willed brat from rural North Central Texas.

Fast forward now to my internship year at the University of Nebraska Medical Center. I am now sitting at the feet of Dr. Charles Golden, clinical neuropsychologist extraordinaire. By the age of 33,

Dr. Golden had produced his own neuropsychologic test battery – widely used around the country – not to mention literally scores of book and journal publications.

Charlie, as he allowed us to call him, was one of the most grating, oppositional individuals you or I will ever meet. A widely feared and anticipated occurrence, the new intern or post-doc – upon initially starting Charlie's rotation – would be subjected to an incredible barrage of verbal vitriol.

I vividly recall mine.

The year was 1982. After being under Dr. Golden's supervision for less than a week, he left town to do a seminar in Chicago. In the meantime, I had two main responsibilities: (1) perform an initial work-up on each new adult inpatient admitted to the Medical Center's Nebraska Psychiatric Institute (NPI); and (2) master the testing system Charlie had authored in 1981, the Luria-Nebraska Neuropsychological Battery (LNNB).

Well, the week I started the rotation, we had approximately twenty persons admitted to NPI's inpatient unit. Each work-up required, on average, 7 hours. Add another 40 hours to learn the LNNB. Now tack on 4 hours of sleep per night, for a sum of 28 hours sack-time for the week. The above comes to a total of 208 hours.

Only one problem. A week contains but 168 hours.

Nevertheless, I thought I was doing great, completing all twenty new admissions – on schedule! Although I hadn't had time to master the intricacies of the LNNB during that week, Charlie would understand, given the overflowing cornucopia of new folks recently added to our inpatient unit.

I was wrong.

Charlie didn't understand.

At all.

Long story painful, at our first group supervision, the good Dr. Golden lit into me with the ferocity of an inflamed grizzly going for fresh meat. In front of everyone. Yes, I had completed all the new patient work-ups; however, I had *not* yet learned his test battery.

But you know what? I didn't care about the verbal tongue-lashing in front of two other faculty supervisors, three interns, and four post-docs. Why? Because I knew this man had knowledge that I needed. So if I could simply withstand the interpersonal ballistics, invaluable information could be mine. And although he would sooner bite a pig than admit it, this man cared about us as trainees. Yes, he was a far cry from the kindly Bill Whitehouse, M.D. But, Dr. Golden cared – whether he would ever fess up to it or not.

Due to people such as Bill and Charlie – polar opposites they – my motivation to succeed jumped exponentially.

So, mentors come in all shapes, sizes, and temperaments. Just be sure you expose Marvin to as many of them as you can.

Motivating Marvin

Part VI

Marvin Under the Microscope

Chapter 32

Marvin's Neuropsychologic Evaluation

Here is Marvin's NP report.

Neuropsychologic Evaluation

NAME: Marvin Doe

AGE: 13 years – 11 months   **DOB:** 2/20/89   GRADE: 8th

DATE OF EVALUATION: 1/11/03

Reason for Referral

Marvin exhibits significant academic underachievement, oppositionalism, externalization of blame, impulsivity, low self-esteem, "nervous" mannerisms, and poor attention/concentration. The patient has received no counseling to date. A neuropsychologic evaluation is needed in order to clarify the differential diagnoses and assist in treatment planning.

Procedures

Lateral Dominance Examination	Gordon Diagnostic System
Bender Visual-Motor Gestalt Test	Attention Deficit Hyperactivity Weighting Scale
Trail Making Test	Selective Verbal Learning Test
Wechsler Intelligence Scale for Children—III	Abstract Visual Memory Test
Woodcock-Johnson Tests of Achievement – Revised	Littauer Personality Profile
Gray Writing Samples Test	Personality Inventory of Children
Stroop Color-Word Test	Randolph Attachment Disorder Questionnaire
Coding—Incidental Learning Test	Thematic Apperception Test—Gray Adaptation
Reitan-Klove Tactile Finger Recognition Test	Rorschach Inkblot Technique
Reitan-Klove Fingertip Number Writing Test	Review of Records
Speech Sounds Perception Test	Parent Interview
Seashore Rhythm Test	Adolescent Interview
Test of Auditory Discrimination	Mental Status

Pertinent History

Marvin is the son of Mr. and Ms. John Doe of Any Town. The current home consists of the patient; Mr. and Ms. Doe; along with Marvin's 15 year-old brother, and 12 year-old sister.

Regarding pre-natal/birth history, such was WNL. Marvin was carried to term, sans delivery complications, with a birth weight of 6 lbs – 11 oz. Developmental milestones included: crawling – 5 months; sitting up – 6 months; first words – 10 months; walking – 11 months; simple sentences – 16 months; and toilet training – 3½ years. The patient's early development is said to have been on par with that of his siblings. In addition, the young man is described as having been a "very compliant, happy, and cuddly" infant, as well as a "very adventurous" toddler.

Medical history is WNL, save for several fractures: left foot (2/98 and 2/02), plus the right clavicle (10/00).

Mental health history is unremarkable. Although Marvin is described as overtly "nervous" at times, he has never been diagnosed with any sort of formalized anxiety disorder. Said nervousness entails worrying about peer acceptance, as well as his parents' safety. The youngster also displays mild facial tics ("twitching") on occasion when under stress. Family mental health history is significant for: anxiety (maternal grandmother); depression (maternal aunt); and R/O ETOH/drug misuse (paternal uncle).

Marvin is enrolled in 8th grade at David B. Stricklin Middle School in Any Town. The youngster is mainstreamed in all classes, while receiving modified curricula in Language Arts. A history of failing marks began in mid 4th grade, but Marvin has managed to successfully pass each year since then "by the skin of his teeth." One chronic source of irritation to his parents is failure to turn in assignments – either at all, or late. Academically, the young man is also described as exhibiting poor attention/concentration, not to mention impulsivity.

As to peer/sibling interaction, the patient is said to display extreme competitiveness – "Marvin always wants to be better than others." The youth is also described as small for his age.

In terms of parent/child relationships, Marvin is perceived as bonded with both Mr. and Ms. Doe. He does, on the other hand, frequently express self-pity – "I'm a horrible person." As to Mr. Doe, the patient is said to be more overtly respectful; however, passive-aggressive behavior is common with both parents (mainly chronic lollygagging and complaining). Additionally, Marvin can be mouthy and directly oppositional – with temper explosions.

Disciplinary techniques utilized include: early bedtime – ineffective, as well as grounding and loss of privileges – both with only mixed efficacy.

The young man has his own bedroom, with no sleep disturbances. As to appetite/eating habits, Marvin is described as "picky."

Extracurricular activities include: movies, computer games, sports, bike riding, and roller-blading. The young man also attends Sunday School/church, wherein he experiences occasional spats with other youth.

Current Medications
None

Previous Medications
None

Mental Status

Marvin is a handsome 13 year – 11 month-old Caucasian male, appearing somewhat younger than his stated age. The lad is of diminutive build, with straight light brown hair – cut in Dutch-boy style, and hazel eyes. He is dressed in green T-shirt with *Nike* screened across the front, green shorts, and white athletic shoes.

Testing begins at 9:10 a.m., with several brief procedures prior to the WJ-R (assessing academic skills). Motoric activity is age-appropriate. Eye contact/speech articulation are WNL. Attention/concentration are likewise WNL. Mood presents as overtly euthymic, with bright affect. Attitude is polite and cooperative. Upon completion of the WJ-R, six tests measuring ADHD are completed.

Subsequent to a 35-minute lunch break, the WISC-III (gauging cognitive factors/IQ) is conducted. We continue with the GWST, two memory tests, the TAT-GA, and lastly a Rorschach.

Marvin is obviously a bright young man who appears to be of solid Above Average range God-given/genetic verbal intelligence. He seems to enjoy the individualized attention of the male examiner. The youngster also clearly relishes the opportunity to construct various geometric patterns on my magnet-board, while the two of us talk during the clinical interview phase of his evaluation.

The youth states that his best friend is Bert, telling that the two reciprocate with sleep-overs – indicating that TV, *X-Box*, and board games are preferred activities on such occasions.

At school, the young man describes his teachers as "O.K.," but that some are "mean." Elaborating, he tells that several are "too strict." As to Marvin's stated reasons for his abundance of MIA daily work papers, he indicates a tendency on his part for "forgetting" to turn them in, acknowledging that such hurts his grades.

Pertaining to family, Marvin tells that his dad is employed "at a company"– frequently able to work from home, and that his mother is a part-time nurse. As for siblings, the youngster cites no unusual conflicts or issues.

The evaluation concludes at 3:45 PM.

Previous Test Results
None

Current Test Results

Lateral Dominance

	Motor Praxis Items	Extremities	Preference
1/03	7 out of 10	Right Upper/Lower (Handwriting – Left)	Mixed Lateral Dominance

Bender-Gestalt

	Errors	Visual-Motor Integration Age	Chronologic Age	Delay	Markers
1/03	0	Age-Appropriate	13 years – 10 months	None	Collisions (1) – Right Anterior Figure Disorganization – Right Anterior

Trail Making

	Part A				Part B			
	Seconds	**Errors**	**Range**	**Markers**	**Seconds**	**Errors**	**Range**	**Markers**
1/03	25	0	> 17 seconds = Impaired	R/O Anxiety	32	1	> 36 seconds = Impaired	WNL

WISC-III

	IQ	Range	Percentile
Verbal Scale	90	Average	25
Performance Scale	102	Average	55
Full Scale	95	Average	37

129

WISC-III continued:

Verbal	SS	IQ Equivalent	Performance	SS	IQ Equivalent
Information	9	95	Picture Completion	12	114
Similarities	9	95	Coding/Digit Symbol	9	95
Arithmetic	9	95	Picture Arrangement	10	100
Vocabulary	8	90	Block Design	10	100
Comprehension	6	75	Object Assembly	10	100
Digit Span	6	75			

Woodcock-Johnson Revised

	Grade Equivalent	Standard Score	Percentile
Word Identification (reading recognition)	9.7	106	65
Word Attack (phonics)	4.9	93	31
Passage Comprehension (reading comprehension)	8.3	98	46
Calculation (computational math)	10.7	108	71
Applied Problems (math story problems)	8.7	99	48
Punctuation/Capitalization Knowledge	6.3	93	32
Spelling/Sight-Word Vocabulary	4.7	84	15
Verb/Noun Usage	5.4	89	22

Gray Writing Samples

	Errors/Markers
Spelling	5
Letter Reversals	0
Capitalization	7
Spacing	6
Punctuation	0
Sentence Run-ons	0
Sentence Fragments	1
Verb/Noun Usage	2
Carelessness	9
Graphics	Average
Left-Right Droop	Mild
Content	Average
Grade Level	Early 8th Grade

Coding – Incidental Learning

Paired Associate Symbol Recall

	Raw Score	Range	Markers
1/03	14 out of 18	Mean = 11.24, SD = 4.16	WNL

Free Recall

	Raw Score	Range	Markers
1/03	7 out of 9	Mean = 7.80, SD = 1.08	WNL

Paired Associate Digit Recall

	Raw Score	Range	Markers
1/03	14 out of 18	Mean = 10.90, SD = 4.64	WNL

Stroop

	Word	Color	Color-Word	Range	Markers
1/03	45	45	46	Mean = 50, SD = 10	WNL

Tactile Finger Recognition

	Right Hand	Left Hand	Range	Markers
1/03	1	1	$\geq$ 4 total = Impaired	WNL

Fingertip Number Writing

	Right Hand	Left Hand	Range	Markers
1/03	2	1	$\geq$ 4 total = Impaired	WNL

Speech Sounds

	Errors	Range	Markers
1/03	8	> 10 errors = Impaired	WNL

Seashore Rhythm

	Correct	Range	Markers
1/03	25	< 24 correct = Impaired	WNL

TAD

Quiet Subtest

	Errors	Percentile	Standard Score	Range	Markers
1/03	1	63rd	105	Average	WNL

Noise Subtest

	Errors	Percentile	Standard Score	Range	Markers
1/03	8	63rd	105	Average	WNL

Gordon

Delay Subtest

	Efficiency Ratio	Total Correct
1/03	.96 (WNL)	30 (Abnormal)

Vigilance Subtest

	Total Commissions	Total Correct
1/03	2 (WNL)	43 (WNL)

Distractibility Subtest

	Total Commissions	Total Correct
1/03	17 (Abnormal)	16 (Abnormal)

Selective Verbal Learning

	Standard Score	Percentile	IQ Equivalent	Range	Markers
1/03	11	63rd	110	Above Average	WNL

133

Abstract Visual Memory

	Standard Score	Percentile	IQ Equivalent	Range	Markers
1/03	9	37th	95	Average	WNL

Attention Deficit Hyperactivity Weighting Scale

Modality	Weighting	Modality	Weighting
TESTING SESSION		**GORDON**	
Fidgets/Impulsive		Delay	1
Motoric Over-Activity		Vigilance	
Poor Attention		Distractibility	1
SCHOOL SETTING		Commission Errors	3
Fidgets/Impulsive	2	**TAD**	
Motoric Over-Activity		Quiet	
Poor Attention	2	Distractibility	2
PIC		**STROOP**	
ADHD	1	Word	
LITTAUER		Color	
Primary Sanguine		Color-Word	
Secondary Sanguine	1	**SPEECH SOUNDS**	
WISC-III		Distractibility	
Arithmetic		**SEASHORE RHYTHM**	
Digit Span	1	Distractibility	2
Coding		**REITAN-KLOVE**	
Picture Completion		Distractibility	
		Distractibility	
		TOTAL	16

RAW SCORE		RANGE
0 – 12	=	WNL
13 – 16	=	**Mild Range**
17 – 20	=	Moderate Range
21 – ↑	=	Severe Range

134

Cerebral Cortex Localization

Left Hemisphere   Right Hemisphere

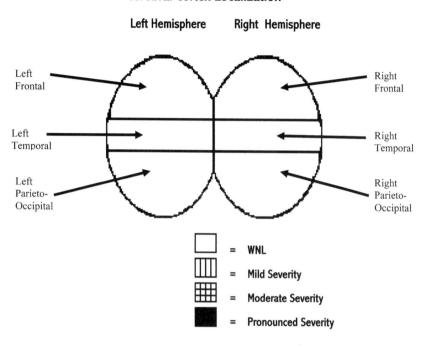

Left Frontal

Right Frontal

Left Temporal

Right Temporal

Left Parieto-Occipital

Right Parieto-Occipital

☐	= WNL
▥	= Mild Severity
▦	= Moderate Severity
■	= Pronounced Severity

Littauer

	Primary	Secondary
1/03	Choleric	Sanguine

TAT-GA

100% → Punitive Consequences *Hit Rate*		
< **90**% → Punitive Consequences *Hit Rate* = abnormal range		
R/O STD	x	**0**
R/O Histrionics	x	**4**
R/O Depression	x	**0**
R/O Psychosexual Aggression	x	**0**
R/O Denial	x	**1**

135

RADQ

	Raw Score	Range	Markers
1/03	50	> 65 = RAD	WNL

PIC

T-Scores		20	30	40	50	60	70	80	90	100	110	120
		Normal Range						**Abnormal Range**				
L				38								
F	"Parental Drain"				54							
DEF	Indices		37									
ADJ									91			
ACH						61						
IS	Learning Triad				56							
DVL				46								
SOM	Histrionics					66						
D	Adolescent Depression					69						
FAM	FOO Conflict		43									
DLQ	Narcissism								90			
WDL	Atypical Depression				54							
ANX	Anxiety/Insecurity					69						
PSY	Borderline Condition				57							
HPR	ADHD							87				
SSK	Social Skills				59							
T-Scores		20	30	40	50	60	70	80	90	100	110	120

Super-Ego Structure

<u>**85**</u>% → Super-Ego/*Conscience* Index
< <u>90</u>% → Super-Ego/*Conscience* Index = abnormal range
40% - 75% → Super-Ego Structure (*Conscience*) Underdevelopment
· Frequently correlates with Narcissism
· 95% probability of full development with proper treatment
0% - 39% → "Absent" Super-Ego Structure (*Conscience*)
· Frequently correlates with Sociopathy
(a total absence of *conscience*)

Rorschach

X-	= .23	(>.33 = abnormal range)	Mild Perceptual Distortion
X+	= .45	(<.45 = abnormal range)	Mild Perceptual Distortion
Populars	= 3 **	(< 5 = abnormal range)	Mild Perceptual Distortion
M-	= 0	(≥ 1 = abnormal range)	Mild Perceptual Distortion
SS	= 6	(≥ 8 = abnormal range)	Subtle Thought Disorder
Fr	= 0	(≥ 1 = abnormal range)	Narcissism
AG	= 3 **	(≥ 2 = abnormal range)	Narcissism
Mor	= 3 **	(≥ 2 = abnormal range)	Depression
C′	= 2 **	(≥ 2 = abnormal range)	Depression
V	= 0	(≥ 1 = abnormal range)	Depression
m	= 7 **	(≥ 2 = abnormal range)	Anxiety
Y	= 1	(≥ 2 = abnormal range)	Anxiety
Sx	= 0	(≥ 2 = abnormal range)	Psychosexual Maladjustment

* Borderline Range
** Clinically Significant Range

Adolescent Bipolar Disorder

1. Borderline Syndrome of Childhood (BSC)	
2. Borderline Psychosis of Childhood (BPC)	
3. Sufficient Neuropsychologic Markers	
4. Documentable Emotionality via Psychometric Data	✓
5. Rapid Daily Cycling/Mood Swings	
6. Chronic Irritability	
7. Parental History of Bipolar Disorder	

1/WNL				
0	—	3	=	WNL
4	—	↑	=	Strong Bipolar Likelihood

Diagnostic Impressions

AXIS I: 300.02   Generalized Anxiety Disorder with mild Atypical Depressive features
        314.01   Attention Deficit Hyperactivity Disorder, mild
        312.90   Disruptive Behavior Disorder
        V62.3   Academic Problem

AXIS II: Narcissistic and Histrionic Traits

AXIS III: Fracture of Left Foot (2/98 and 2/02), by history
Fracture of Clavicle (10/00), by history

AXIS IV: Psychosocial Stressors: Academic underachievement

AXIS V: Current GAF: 55

Treatment Options

(1) First of all, I would check with Dr. Pediatrician regarding a trial on a psychostimulant for Marvin – such as Ritalin, Dexedrine, Adderall, etc. Currently, the youth tests out with an ADHD Weighting Scale raw score of 16/Mild range. Getting Marvin's ADHD symptomatology neutralized should make a huge difference in his overall behavior (not just in terms of his ability to concentrate and pay attention at school and with homework). However, I respectfully bow to Dr. Pediatrician here.

(2) Next, given the Generalized Anxiety Disorder with mild features of atypical depression, I recommend we also check with Dr. Pediatrician regarding a trial on a low-dose SSRI agent. Such would of course be subsequent to getting Marvin squared away on the most appropriate psychostimulant, at optimal dosage, should Mr. and Ms. Doe feel a peace with this.

(3) I also recommend EEG Neurofeedback (NFB) for Marvin. Every year more research data emerge demonstrating the efficacy of brain re-training – whereby actual neurologic electrical function is optimized and regulated – often with excellent results in terms of ADHD, anxiety, and depression. Such would not however remove consideration for psychopharmacology – at least within the short term. However, it is my experience that once EEG NFB training is performed, a youngster's need for psychotropic medications is decreased, and in many instances no longer needed. Information regarding EEG NFB can be found at www.eegspectrum.com.

(4) Given Marvin's prominent Choleric temperament, Dobson's book, *The New Strong-Willed Child*, merits a review by Mr. and Ms. Doe. However, Marvin's super-ego structure (conscience) tests out at almost WNL status – obviously a good sign.

(5) Regarding behavioral interventions utilized within the home, Marvin receives early bedtime – ineffective, as well as grounding/loss of privileges – the latter consisting of spotty efficacy at best. With similar Choleric/strong-willed kiddoes, the foundational bedrock of any disciplinary approach is going to be the systematic nuking of TVG (*Toxic Verbal Gameyness*).

Although I can't speak for Mr. and Ms. Doe, most parents in our culture choose to lecture…explain…pontificate…debate…re-explain…and spell out expectations over and over and over to our youth – as if they have experienced a stroke – replete with pronounced memory loss – since the last time we enumerated rules for them, 10 minutes earlier! Such only serves to elevate a kiddo's inappropriate power-base within the home.

Explain what we expect once – maybe twice. Then don't get sucked into more of this. Be *Navy Seal* parents during periods of discipline. Get in and get *out*.

(6) Moreover, I recommend Mr. and Ms. Doe check out Dr. Kenneth Kaye's *Family Rules* Chapter 8: "The Art of Grounding." Such is short/easy to read, providing effective pointers as to how we as parents can use grounding and restriction of privileges in the most effective manner with our youth.

(7) We should also give thought to utilization of *Audio Therapy*. Such entails using a small/inexpensive micro-cassette recorder to capture episodes of verbal sassing on the part of Marvin. Then, such can be immediately, or later on, played back for him to hear. It's very important though that such be done in a subtly jocular/low-key fashion by parents.

(8) Furthermore, Mr. and Ms. Doe should consider Videocam Therapy. The way this works is that we calmly explain to Marvin that the household has been asked by Steven Spielberg to provide celluloid vignettes for possible usage in the upcoming horror/comedy, *The Wolfman Meets Bill Clinton* – starring Denzel Washington, Jim Carrey, and Billy Bob Thornton – with a brief cameo appearance by Whoopi Goldberg.

We then keep our little camcorder within easy reach at home. On occasions wherein the young man begins to argue, spit, curse, or fume – we merely roll camera. Later on, at a time convenient for the parents, a sneak-preview of the film is served up for any interested family members to watch. Provide soft drinks, Jolly Ranchers, popcorn, and dill pickles for all. Moreover, it isn't necessary that Marvin be present at the time of viewing. However, curiosity usually gets the best of young persons here.

Oh, and don't forget to keep parental tongues planted firmly in cheek with this procedure also.

(9) Mr. and Ms. Doe should furthermore consider Bland Sandwich Therapy, whereby Marvin would be required – on days of restricted privileges – to eat a sandwich brought from home (e.g., a plain-Jane concoction consisting of, say, a slice of tomato, clump of lettuce, and dab of Grey Poupon) – as opposed to being allowed to choose an item from the menu, should the family be dining/doing carry-out at a pizza place, fast food joint, etc.

(10) Furthermore, I recommend we set Marvin up on a Motivation Plan (MP) at some point prior to 9th grade. An MP is a structured format coordinated by parents, to inject a daily dosage of academic *MO* into a young person, in order to nuke MIA homework, as well as academic under-production.

It's my experience that once we begin to incorporate an MP, an elevation in self-esteem almost always occurs on the part of the young person – along with improved grades. And, our clinic can set this up for Mr. and Ms. Doe, via a single 2-hour session, with prn follow-up.

(11) This youth will also profit from a weekly 60-minute session of outside professional tutoring over the summer, leading into 9th grade, targeting the lean punctuation/capitalization skills and overall compositional writing. Aside from the embolsterment of these deficiencies, tutoring will also help Marvin develop what I call *academic moxie*. The latter will only however be achieved as long as the tutor is someone with whom the teen can relate, via a mentoring scenario.

(12) Finally, I would be honored to provide a follow-up neuropsychologic exam at any point in the future for Marvin, should the need arise. He wouldn't likely need a full evaluation, only a partial. At any rate, the current work-up will serve as an excellent baseline for subsequent comparison.

My best wishes to Marvin. Thank you very much for allowing me to evaluate this young man. I hope the information is helpful to him, Mr. and Ms. Doe, David B. Stricklin Middle School, and Dr. Pediatrician.

Steven G. Gray, Ph.D.
Steven G. Gray, Ph.D.
Diplomate, American Board of Pediatric Neuropsychology
Diplomate, American Board of Vocational Neuropsychology
Clinical Assistant Professor, The University of Texas Southwestern
     Medical Center

Chapter 33

Marvin's Motivation Plan

The following is Marvin's MP. By the way, it generally takes an additional 2-hour visit with the young man's parents – following completion of the neuropsychologic evaluation/feedback session – to set up the MP.

The Complete Process

Step 1	Neuropsychologic Examination	6-7 hours
Step 2	Scoring and Analysis of Tests	4 days
Step 3	Generating Parent's Report	4 days
Step 4	Parent Feedback Session	3-3½ hours
Step 5	Motivation Plan Development	2 hours
Step 6	Presenting Plan to Marvin	½ hour

Figure 33.1   The Complete Process

This MP planning session is done with Mom and Dad only. Marvin doesn't attend this meeting. Then, it is usually advisable that a half-hour follow-up session is done, on a separate day, subsequent to the parents and I getting the MP established. Here, we explain the MP to Marvin, and invite him to make suggestions, which his parents and I listen to.

Daily Schedule

With Marvin, due to Mom's part-time work schedule, as well as Dad's job flexibility (the freedom to do a portion of work from his office at home), both parents shared the responsibilities of implementing the young man's MP – depending on the particular day of the week. Dad had Mondays and Wednesdays; Mom – Tuesdays and Thursdays. See Marvin's Motivation Plan schemata below.

A United Front

One of the tricks to working out an MP with Marvin was to first create the needed Vulcan Mind-meld vis-à-vis his parents. Dad was something of a drill sergeant type. Mom was more the empathic counselor type. Fortunately, to the credit of Mom and Dad, they were able to reach common ground in terms of an MP modus operandi – once their differing parenting styles were examined and discussed. For more on the United Front, see Chapter 16.

Parent-Teacher Conduit

Another strength that Marvin's situation served up was a very tight Parent-Teacher Conduit. This young man's school district had recently implemented an on-line computer generation (updated every Friday), including the status of students' daily-work papers, test grades, and weekly grade average – for each subject.

This was *huge*.

Either Marvin or his parents could pull up on a 24/7 basis what was happening in any of his classes. By the way, I highly recommend such a computerized system for every school district in America.

Motivation Plan Schemata for Marvin

Schedule*		Parent-School Conduit*	Carrots/Sticks*
7:20	School Begins	▷ Regular In-person Parent-Teacher Conference (once per term) ▷ Parent INTOUCH (access to grades via Internet)	▷ Snacks
2:20	Out of School	▷ Weekly E-mail from teachers	▷ Choice of Week-end Family Activity
3:00	Arrives Home	▷ E-mailing teachers, as needed	▷ Verbal Praise/ Recognition
3:15	Snack/Free-time	▷ Phone Calls/Meetings with teachers, as needed	▷ TV Access
4:15	Homework		▷ Attendance at Out-of-State Family Wedding
4:30	Dad Home/ Debriefed by Marvin		▷ Acquisition of Cell-Phone
	Look through Assignments		▷ Trip to Mall/Video Store
	Homework		▷ Guitar Lessons
6:30	Dinner		
7:00			▷ Sleep-over with Friend
7:30	Homework/Study for Tests (If Marvin completes homework around 8:00 p.m. ish, he earns TV/ video games/ guitar access)		▷ Computer-Game Access
8:30	Shower/Snack/ Free-time		
9:00	Bed-time		

* Each of the three columns is independent of one another. Not to be read horizontally.

Figure 33.2 Marvin's Motivation Plan Schemata

In addition, with Marvin – as can be seen from Figure 33.2 of his MP Schemata, other means of parent-teacher communication occurred, by way of e-mails, phone calls, three or four sit-down conferences with teachers during the school year, as well as prn (as needed) pow-wows. Clearly, Marvin's situation offered him a very robust Parent-Teacher Conduit.

By the way, one of the aspects I always like to look at in helping a family work up an MP is, "Worst-case scenario, what are your **fears** – should he continue along in DU La-La Land?" In this regard, Dad's concerns consisted of Marvin: (1) not being able to attend college; (2) continuing down his present road of bargain-basement academic ambition; and (3) growing into the same sort of adult as Marvin's uncle – a man who never really found a steady vocation, aimlessly drifting from job to job throughout his life – outwardly manifesting little vocational ambition.

Mom's dreads for Marvin were: (1) that he would miss out on a college education; (2) that her son would never find his vocational niche in life; and (3) that he wouldn't be *happy* as an adult.

I think it's really important to allow parents of DUs to explore and talk about their greatest fears for their underachieving youngster. There is a decided catharsis in doing this, which helps Mom and Dad face up to what indeed is their greatest disappointment angst, regarding Marvin. As I stated back in Chapter 8, a typical unspoken/non-conscious concern on the part of parents is that their kiddo will never grow up.

Emotional Climate of the Home

Marvin was quite the skilled *baiter* – especially with Dad. The young man's hit parade of verbal/non-verbal barbs are included in Figure 33.3 below.

Marvin's Greatest Hits

- ▶ The *You Don't Trust Me! Mantra*
- ▶ The Marvin *Dopey Look*
  (when confronted with errors in homework)
- ▶ The Marvin *Stone-Face Look*
  (when confronted with errors with sloppy homework)
- ▶ The *I Don't Need to Check Over That Again! Assertion*,
  vis-à-vis homework.
- ▶ The *Race Through Assignments MO* complete with
  an apparent attitude of, "I really couldn't give a dad gum
  rip-roar about this – I just want to finish. O.K.?!"

Figure 33.3 Marvin's Greatest Hits

At any rate, needless to say, all of the above set the stage for a decided scratchy emotionality within the home, surrounding Marvin's nightly escapade of Homework Hell.

One of the strategies we therefore used in dealing with this was to first help Dad become aware that his son was indeed a highly skilled baiter (rated an 8.5 out of 10 by the Ukrainian judge). And, I have to say – Dad did a great job of backing off of Marvin's goads, not permitting himself – after a time – to become sucked into these any longer.

Moreover, it goes without saying that TVG oozed out of the walls, surrounding Marvin's after-school homework drudgery. So, Mom, Dad, and I needed to broach this situation as well. Again, they were both receptive and very effective with this. I also spoke with Mr. and Ms. Doe about the need to become Navy Seal Parents (see Chapter 22).

In addition, Dr. Sylvia Rimm's concept of Referential Speaking (see Chapter 17) was helpful with Marvin. Suffice it to say, this teen hadn't heretofore given his folks many opportunities for Referential Speaking.

Bite-Size is Better

As all parents of DUs painfully realize, school projects/written work constitute one of the most aversive situations confronting them. Such is akin to having bamboo shoots laced with ammonia inserted into one's fingernails. Having a research project or long written assignment, within the context of a DU, is similar to simultaneously having a root canal along with a colonoscopy – both without anesthesia.

So, to deal with research papers and/or lengthy written compositions, we needed to go back to the late 60s wherein the old Slice'n Dice kitchen appliance was faddish. You know, that culinary aide which chops up vegetables at warp speed. (By the way, Dad, I don't recommend one of these as an anniversary gift for your wife. Trust me on this. But, I digress once again…)

Anyway, I'm talking about a metaphorical Slice'n Dice. That is, dividing up long school assignments – the research project, the term paper, etc, etc, etc. Little successes lead to big successes (Teaff, 1994). Whittling up writing assignments into manageable parts is especially effective among youth (Feifer & De Fina, 2002).

Here, we sit down with Marvin, helping him chop up said marathon task into bite-size portions – beginning with an overall outline of the entire enchilada. In this way, he can begin to get the feel of a divide and conquer mentality – a skill, by the way, which will last him the rest of his earthly life.

Next, get a simple kitchen timer. Use it to set short-term goals. This is a technique we used with our own son, Forrest, as he was growing up. "O.K., Forrest, let's set the timer for 30 minutes. Think you can pull up off the internet and read through six items from it on your Ireland Project, in – say – 30 minutes? You *do*? O.K., great! I'll be back in 30 minutes, when the buzzer goes off. After that, you can take a 15 minute break for free-time."

148

Then, we would continue on in this fashion – using the bite-size slice'n dice method – until completion of the project. As Forrest got older, he gradually learned to take on more and more of the bite-size slice'n dice on his own, with less and less involvement from me or my wife, Debbi.

Remember, it's the human pre-frontal lobes that serve as the CEO of the brain – organizing, planning, and making wise decisions. The younger the child – the more he will need provision of prosthetic pre-frontal lobes. Who, in the early going, acts as prostheses? Right. We do, the parents. As Marvin's brain gradually matures and bakes out over the years, he needs less and less prostheses. Said another way – unless you have a highly precocious child – simply turning over a long/convoluted research project, pell-mell, to a 10 or 11 year-old is tantamount to psychosis.

Carrots

For our man, Marvin, see Figure 33.2 on his MP schemata, as to what sort of rewards held the greatest valence for him. Example: he rated money, snacks, his choice of a week-end family activity, TV access, and being allowed to attend a cousin's out of state wedding 4 months away, as most potent privileges.

Items of lesser value included: acquisition of a cell-phone, trips to the mall/video store, continued guitar lessons, verbal praise, having a friend for a nocturnal stay-over, and computer-game access.

By the way, once Marvin's parents and I set up the MP plan, we then met with him on a separate day, for purposes of eliciting what privileges held highest allure for *him*. This is the half-hour follow-up session I referred to in Figure 33.1 on the first page of this chapter. Caveat: not infrequently, we adults misjudge which perks and rewards are most important to kiddoes. Thus, the moral, concerning earned rewards: ask Marvin.

So, the laundry list of possible carrots included: (1) short-range (e.g., daily TV access); (2) mid-range (e.g., choice of week-end family activity); to (3) long-range (e.g., attendance of cousin's out-of-state wedding). See Figure 33.4 to find out what Marvin actually had to do in order to obtain the short-, mid-, and long-range rewards he had identified for himself. (By the way, the young man's parents weren't comfortable with the notion of giving Marvin monetary carrots. Some Moms and Dads are O.K. with this, including the author. However, some aren't, and that's fine.)

Short-Range	Mid-Range	Long-Range
Getting all homework done, and checked by a parent, making any needed corrections. If so, was released to free-time until 9 p.m. lights-out.	No *MIA* homework papers or failing grades for a given week. **If** none, had choice of having a friend stay over on Friday night, choosing a week-end family activity, etc.	All Bs-Cs on final year-end semester averages. If so, could attend out-of-state wedding with rest of family in early June.

Figure 33.4 Marvin's Carrot Criteria

Sticks

In the main, an implementation of sticks for Marvin simply canceled out many of the possible carrots he was able to earn. Figure 33.5 below delineated the teen's stick scenarios.

So, this is what we set up for Marvin in terms of an MP. Via a team approach (the teen, his parents, teachers, and me), I'm happy to report that this young man, with a several-year history of academic underachievement, pulled his grades up by the end of the semester to all A's and B's.

150

Short-Range	Mid-Range	Long-Range
Lollygagging on homework, or verbal sassing. Such simply ate up more of his daily after-school free-time (i.e., less free-time prior to lights-out – meaning little or no phone/TV/ computer-game access for the evening).	An *MIA* homework paper or failing grade during the week. Such precluded any week-end sleep-overs/choices of family fun, etc.	Any failing final year-end semester grade below a C. Such precluded his attending out-of-state wedding with rest of family – as well as reimbursing parents for the $100.00 penalty related to not using advance-booked airline ticket for said wedding.

Figure 33.5 Marvin's *Stick* Criteria

By the way, I attended Marvin's middle school graduation ceremony in early June. The young man was beaming, with a distinct aura of satisfaction and accomplishment on his face as he walked down to get his diploma.

By the way #2, Marvin's mom called me on the phone over a year later at which point the youth had completed 9th grade. She was very pleased to report that Marvin had maintained his good grades throughout the difficult first year of high school.

Chapter 34

Some Final Thoughts

I suppose my main goal in writing this book is to give hope. To parents and all Marvins everywhere. But remember, nothing worth a plug nickel is achieved without elbow grease.

The same is true for helping transform a DU into an IA. So, folks, proceed with diligence, patience, and confidence.

For Christian parents, remember too that our timing is very rarely God's timing. Accordingly, during the next occasion of discouragement about Marvin's academic progress (or apparent lack of same), take heart! Remember, *God is in control, and He knows what He's doing*. Anyone can quit. Anyone can take the easy path.

The example of Roy Sunada serves us well in this regard. Mr. Sunada is the advanced placement coordinator for John Marshall Fundamental Secondary School in Pasadena, California. At John Marshall, more than 70% of the students are minority – 60% qualify for free/reduced-price lunches.

In the 6 years under Mr. Sunada's charge, the number of students passing AP courses has skyrocketed from 37 in 1997, to 187 in 2003. Currently, nearly 33% of Marshall attendees are enrolled in AP – strenuous courses that earn collegiate credits provided that the final exam is passed. Moreover, during this same 6-year window, the percentage of Marshall graduates attending college has gone from 57% to 88%.

Roy Sunada is a teacher who believes all kids – even those from financially disadvantaged backgrounds – can succeed academically. A tough taskmaster, Mr. Sunada demands effort on the part of his students. He exhorts young people to push themselves. And to believe in themselves.

Also consider Dr. Ben Carson. At Johns Hopkins since 1984, this man – no different from Roy Sunada – is an Olympic-class role model for youth everywhere.

Ben Carson grew up in Detroit and Boston, beset by poverty. Early on, his grades in school were abysmal. Anger and a cellar-dweller self-esteem weighted him down. Via the firm hand of his mother, Ben decided to change his life direction, from academic failure to academic achiever.

Within 18 months, this young/impoverished African-American boy, began ingesting book after book – working his way up from 5th grade academic tree-stump, to the top of his 7th grade class. Dr. Carson quips that his school transformation was so dramatic during this time in his life that onlookers probably suspected he had undergone a brain transplant!

In actuality, young Ben had managed to alter his own self-perception and revamp the expectations he held for himself. Reading biographies of successful people was key. He also pooh-poohed nay-sayers along the way who attempted to derail his dreams of becoming a physician. Dr. Carson also hugely credits his mother who enthusiastically encouraged reading – although she never learned herself. As a result of her unending emotional support, Ben Carson learned first-hand what personal discipline and effort could achieve.

I believe it worked. Dr. Carson is today the world's pre-eminent pediatric neurosurgeon.

Like Roy Sunada and Ben Carson, all of us can serve as enthusiastic role models for young people. It is my belief that God only holds us as parents accountable for what we can control. Therefore, if we do our best in raising our kids, that is all God will ask. I simply cannot imagine Him holding us liable for how our youth ultimately turn out – only were we faithful, and did we do what He asked of us. Beyond that, rest in Him.

> *Therefore having been justified by faith, we have peace with God through our Lord Jesus Christ...We take extreme joy in our tribulations, knowing that tribulation brings about perseverance; and perseverance, proven character; and proven character, hope.* Romans 5:1-4

Peace, perseverance, and hope. My prayer is that this book encourages all three for you and Marvin.

Motivating Marvin

Part VII

End Notes

Appendix I

Common Abbreviations/Acronyms

AA – Alcoholics Anonymous
AD – Attachment Disorder
ADD – Attention Deficit Disorder
ADHD – Attention Deficit Hyperactivity Disorder
ADHD-WS – Attention Deficit Hyperactivity Disorder Weighting Scale
AP – advanced placement
ARD – Admission, Review, and Dismissal
ATTACh – Association for Treatment and Training in the Attachment of Children
BC – Borderline Condition
BD – Bipolar Disorder
BDA – Borderline Disorder of Adolescence
BDC – Borderline Disorder of Childhood
bid – twice per day
BP – Borderline Psychosis
BPA – Borderline Psychosis of Adolescence
BPC – Borderline Psychosis of Childhood
BPD – Borderline Personality Disorder
BSA – Borderline Syndrome of Adolescence
BSC – Borderline Syndrome of Childhood
CBD – Childhood Bipolar Disorder
CD – Conduct Disorder
CNS – Central Nervous System
CR – controlled release
DSM-IV – *Diagnostic and Statistical Manual – 4th Edition*
DU – dependent underachiever
ED – emotionally disturbed
EED – Excessive Extracurricular Disorder
EEG – electroencephalograph
EKG – electrocardiograph
ER – extended release
ERS – End-Run Syndrome

FAE – Fetal Alcohol Effects
FAS – Fetal Alcohol Syndrome
FIQ – Full Scale Intelligence
FOO – family of origin
GAD – Generalized Anxiety
    Disorder
GE – grade equivalent
GP – grade placement
GWST – Gray Writing Samples
    Test
IA – Independent Achiever
IDEA – Individuals with
    Disability Education Act
IED – Intermittent Explosive
    Disorder
IEP – Individual Education Plan
IQ – Intelligence Quotient
LD – Learning Disability
LiCo – Lithium Carbonate
LLD – Language Learning
    Disability
LNNB – Luria-Nebraska Neuro-
    psychological Battery
LS – learning style
MDD – Major Depressive
    Disorder
MIA – missing in action
MO – motivation
MP – Motivation Plan
MRI – magnetic resonance
    imaging
NFB – Neurofeedback

NLD – Nonverbal Learning
    Disability
NP – neuropsychologic
NPI – Nebraska Psychiatric
    Institute
OCD – Obsessive-Compulsive
    Disorder
ODD – Oppositional Defiant
    Disorder
PET – Photon Emission
    Tomography
PIC – Personality Inventory for
    Children
PIQ – Performance Scale
    Intelligence Quotient
PTSD – Post-traumatic Stress
    Disorder
qEEG – quantitative EEG
RAD – Reactive Attachment
    Disorder
RADQ – Randolph Attachment
    Disorder Questionnaire
R/O – rule out
Rx – prescription
SNRI – Selective Norepinephrine
    Reuptake Inhibitor
SPECT – Single Photon
    Emission Computerized
    Tomography
SR – sustained release
SS – short and sharp
SSP – study skills program

SSRI – Selective Serotonin Reuptake Inhibitor

TAD – Test of Auditory Discrimination

TAT – Thematic Apperception Test

TAT-GA – Thematic Apperception Test – Gray Adaptation

TFRT – Tactile Finger Recognition Test

TOP – Tack-On Phenomenon

TVG – Toxic Verbal Gameyness

VIQ – Verbal Scale Intelligence Quotient

WAIS-III – Wechsler Adult Intelligence Scale – 3rd Edition

WISC-III – Wechsler Intelligence Scale for Children – 3rd Edition

WJ-R – Woodcock-Johnson – Revised

WNL – within normal limits

WPPSI-III – Wechsler Preschool and Primary Scale of Intelligence

XR – extended release

Appendix II

Glossary

Abstract Visual Memory Test – a standardized visual memory test

Adderall – a psychostimulant medication (used to treat ADHD)

Adderall XR – a psychostimulant medication, extended release version

Affect – demeanor

Ambien – an hypnotic medication (used to treat insomnia)

Amotivation – lack of motivation

Anti-anxiety medications – a class of medications used to treat anxiety

Anti-convulsants – a class of medications known for stabilizing mood, in addition to their anti-seizure properties

Anti-depressants – a class of medications that can elevate mood (used to treat depression)

Anti-psychotics – also known as neuroleptics; a class of medications used to treat various forms of psychoses

Anxiolytics – another name for anti-anxiety medications

Ativan – an anxiolytic medication (used to treat anxiety)

Attention Deficit Disorder (ADD) – the older name for the current diagnosis of ADHD

Attention Deficit Hyperactivity Disorder (ADHD) – a diagnosis characterized by difficulty in sustaining attention, forgetfulness, and/or impulsivity. Hyperactivity may or may not be present

Attention Deficit Hyperactivity Weighting Scale (ADHD-WS) – a diagnostic measure which assesses the presence (or lack of) ADHD

Atypical Anti-psychotics – another name for a newer class of neuroleptic medications (used to treat Borderline Condition/psychoses)

Atypical Depression – a depression which does not display the usual symptoms such as sadness, appetite disturbance, etc.

Behavior Modification – one of a multitude of different programs which reward a child for exhibiting desired actions

Bender Visual-Motor Gestalt Test – a standardized test measuring visual-motor/spatial skills

Beta-blockers – a class of drugs used to treat ADHD, as well as hypertension

Bipolar Disorder (BD) – a syndrome among adults characterized by severe mood swings from elation to deep depression; formerly called Manic-Depressive Illness

Borderline Condition (BC) – a disorder of childhood/adolescence encompassing either Borderline Psychosis or Borderline Syndrome

Borderline Personality Disorder (BPD) – a character disorder wherein severe interpersonal problems, manipulation, irresponsibility, and unstable moods are common

Borderline Psychosis (BP) – an emerging or intermittent struggle with maintaining a clear grasp of reality via mild perceptual distortion, subtle thought disorder, and/or deviant fantasy operations

Borderline Syndrome – a less severe kissing-cousin to Borderline Psychosis

BuSpar – an anxiolytic medication (used to treat anxiety)

C3–C4 – EEG sites along the sensory-motor strip

C3–FP1 – EEG sites located atop the left hemisphere

Celexa – an SSRI anti-depressant medication (used to treat depression)

Central Nervous System (CNS) – made up of the brain and spinal cord

Cerebellum – the portion of the brain just above the brainstem which primarily controls balance and motor coordination

Cerebrum – composed of the pre-frontal, frontal, temporal, parietal, and occipital lobes

Childhood Bipolar Disorder (CBD) – a syndrome characterized by extreme irritability, frequent mood swings, and tantrum activity

Choleric – one of the four personality temperaments – decisive, goal-oriented, strong-willed, natural-born leader

Clonidine – a generic Beta-blocker medication (used to treat ADHD symptoms and/or hypertension)

Clozaril – an atypical anti-psychotic medication (used to treat Borderline Condition/psychoses)

Coding-Incidental Learning Test – a measure used to assess memory function

Cognition – thought

Color-Form Test – a standardized test of cognitive flexibility

Concerta – a psychostimulant medication (used to treat ADHD symptoms)

Concerta XR – a psychostimulant medication – extended release version

Conduct Disorder (CD) – a behavioral disorder among youth wherein aggression, property destruction, stealing, and blatant disregard for others and/or the law are present

Controlled Release (CR) – a medication in which the active ingredients are absorbed into the body at a consistent level

Cortex – the outer layer of the cerebrum, highly developed in humans

Cortical – referring to the cortex of the brain

Cusp – on the border of

Cyclothymia – a cycling of moods similar to adult Bipolar Disorder, but less pronounced

Cylert – a psychostimulant medication (used to treat ADHD symptoms)

De-gaming – a stepping out of repetitive behaviors youth exhibit at home or school

Depakene – an anti-convulsant medication (used to treat Bipolar, seizure disorders, or impulse control syndromes)

Depakote – an anti-convulsant medication (used to treat Bipolar, seizure disorders, or impulse control syndromes)

Dependent Underachiever (DU) – a youngster who academically struggles, despite ability, usually due to learned helplessness

Depression – a diagnosis in which any of the following can occur: psycho-motor retardation/agitation, decreased pleasure in activities, social withdrawal, insomnia, fatigue, appetite suppression/enhancement, notions of worthlessness or guilt, inability to concentrate, and suicidal thoughts

Desyrel – an anti-depressant medication with soporific properties (often used to treat insomnia)

Dexedrine – a psychostimulant medication (used to treat ADHD)

Dextrostat – a combination psychostimulant medication (used to treat ADHD)

Dopamine – one of several neurotransmitters in the brain

Dyscalculia – extreme difficulty involving computational math skills, often due to LD

Dysgraphia – extreme difficulty with motor control, often associated with LD

Dyslexia – an LD involving reading, spelling, and/or writing skills

Dyspraxia – extreme difficulty with motor control, often associated with LD

Dysthymia – a chronic form of depression

Effexor – an anti-depressant medication (used to treat depression)

Effexor XR – an anti-depressant medication, extended release version

Elavil – a tricyclic anti-depressant medication (used to treat depression)

Electrocardiograph (EKG) – a measure of heart activity

Electroencephalograph (EEG) – a measure of brain electrical activity

End-Run Syndrome (ERS) – a youth's effort to undermine parents' attempts to enhance his academic achievement

Endorphins – chemicals within the brain which help elevate mood

Excessive Extracurricular Disorder (EED) – loading down kiddoes with too many after-school activities

Extended Release (XR) – a medication in which the active ingredients are absorbed into the body at a consistent level

Fetal Alcohol Effects (FAE) – symptoms in a child due to the mother's alcohol consumption during pregnancy; not as severe as FAS

Fetal Alcohol Syndrome (FAS) – a syndrome of birth defects, CNS problems, and/or mental retardation resultant to alcohol consumption during pregnancy

Fingertip Number Writing Test – a standardized test measuring attention/concentration

Frontal Lobes – part of the cerebrum, just behind the pre-frontal lobes

Generalized Anxiety Disorder (GAD) – a diagnosis characterized by nonspecific anxiety, involving the autonomic nervous system

Geodon – an atypical anti-psychotic medication (used to treat Borderline Condition/psychoses)

Gordon Diagnostic System – a standardized test assessing visual attention/ concentration

Graphic Dyspraxia – an impairment in the quality of printing/cursive

Gray Writing Samples Test (GWST) – a measure assessing compositional writing skills

Grounding – a disciplinary action which restricts a youth's activities for a specified period of time

Guilt-jerking – a young person's attempt to control his parents via hitting their guilt buttons

Haldol – a neuroleptic medication (used to treat various forms of psychoses)

Hit-Rate – the probability of correctly identifying or diagnosing a specific syndrome or condition

Hyperactivity – excessive motor movement

Hypnotics – a classification of medications used to treat insomnia

Hypomania – a less severe kissing-cousin to mania

Imipramine – a generic form of the tricyclic anti-depressant, Tofranil

Independent Achiever (IA) – a student who successfully manages his own academic workload

Individualized Education Plan (IEP) – an annually reviewed/updated written report via a school system's Special Education department – detailing special services, timelines, and evaluation procedures required by a student with a disability

Intermittent Explosive Disorder (IED) – a brain-based disorder characterized by periodic ballistic episodes

Lamictal – an anti-convulsant medication (used to treat Bipolar, seizure disorders, or impulse control syndromes)

Language Learning Disability (LLD) – a neurologic LD confined to reading, spelling, and/or writing

Lateral Dominance Examination – a test for determining right/left preference

Learning Disability (LD) – a pronounced difficulty processing environmental/academic information

Learning Style (LS) – the manner in which a person comprehends new information (visual, auditory, kinesthetic)

Librium – an anxiolytic medication (used to treat anxiety)

Lifer Syndrome – develops secondary to a youngster being punished for such a long time period that she becomes discouraged, losing all motivation to improve behavior

Lithium Carbonate (LiCo) – a salt (used as a mood stabilizer to treat Bipolar Disorder)

Littauer Personality Profile – a test assessing human temperament

Luvox – an SSRI anti-depressant medication (used to treat depression)

Magnetic Resonance Imaging (MRI) – allows detailed images of the body to be seen via computer

Major Depressive Disorder (MDD) – the most extreme form of depression

Mania – a highly elevated mood, accompanied by frenzied activity

Manic-Depressive Illness – the old term for Bipolar Disorder

Marker – a road-sign frequently characteristic of a specific disorder or syndrome

Masked Depression – a type of depression with manifestations of oppositionalism and rebellion, wherein classic signs of typical depression such as blunted affect, overt sadness, etc are absent

Melancholy – one of the four personality temperaments – usually described as organized and detail-oriented

Mellaril – a neuroleptic medication (used to treat various forms of psychoses)

Metadate – a psychostimulant medication (used to treat ADHD symptoms)

Methylphenidate – the generic form of Ritalin

Minimal Brain Dysfunction (MBD) – an old term indicating mild impairment of brain function

Moban – a neuroleptic medication (used to treat psychoses)

Mood Stabilizer – a psychotropic capable of smoothing out the highs and/or lows of mood

Moxie – charisma, savvy

Navane – a neuroleptic medication (used to treat psychoses)

Neurofeedback (NFB) – measurement/regulation of brain electrical activity

Neuroleptic – another name for anti-psychotic medications

Neuron – brain cells

Neurontin – an anti-convulsant medication (used to treat impulse control disorders)

Neurotransmitters – chemical substances which carry messages between brain cells

Nonverbal Learning Disability (NLD) – an atypical form of LD characterized by deficits in motor coordination, visual-spatial skills, and interpersonal relationships

Norepinephrine – one of several neurotransmitters in the brain

Norpramin – a tricyclic anti-depressant medication (used to treat depression)

Obsessive-Compulsive Disorder (OCD) – extreme ritualistic behavior which interferes with daily living

Occipital Lobe – the portion of the brain at the back of the cerebrum, governing vision

Occupational Therapist (OT) – specializes in helping people develop and recover skills needed for daily living and work, usually via development of the upper extremities

Oppositional Defiant Disorder (ODD) – a disorder defined by extreme hostility/rebellious actions and attitude

Pamelor – a tricyclic anti-depressant medication (used to treat depression)

Panic Attacks – acute episodes of anxiety usually accompanied by increased heart rate, respiration, profuse sweating, and notions of impending doom

Parent Training and Information Center (PTIC) – an agency which helps parents negotiate policies and procedures to ensure the best/most appropriate education for their child

Parentified Child – a youngster who acts as another parent within a family

Parietal Lobes – the region near the back of the cerebrum, performing a large variety of cognitive functions

Parieto-Occipital Region – the area of the cerebrum where the parietal and occipital lobes join

Passive-Aggressive – a chronic syndrome characterized by hidden/under-the-table aggression, as opposed to overt hostility

Paxil – an SSRI anti-depressant medication (used to treat depression)

Peabody Picture Vocabulary Test-III (PPVT-III) – a standardized test measuring receptive language

Performance Scale Intelligence Quotient (PIQ) – a measurement of overall visual-motor/visual-spatial abilities, from the Wechsler IQ tests

Personality Inventory for Children (PIC) – a standardized test measuring psychologic/emotional status

Pervasive Developmental Disorder – a syndrome characterized by a host of concurrent developmental anomalies; a less severe kissing-cousin to Autism

Phlegmatic – one of the four personality temperaments – usually described as *laid back*, sensitive to others, patient, a good listener, shy

Photon Emission Tomography (PET) – an imaging test used in neurology and psychiatry

Polypharmacy – excessive/multiple medications

Post-traumatic Stress Disorder (PTSD) – a syndrome in which one re-experiences traumatic event(s) from the past – with accompanying fears, nightmares, and CNS disturbance

Pre-frontal Lobes – the most forward portion of the frontal lobes, directly behind the forehead – involved in highly complex cognitive processing

Progressive Figures Test – a measure for young children assessing cognitive flexibility

Prozac – an SSRI anti-depressant medication (used to treat depression)

Psychostimulants – a classification of medications which escalate CNS activity, used to treat ADHD

Psychotropics – medications used for mental health purposes

Quantitative Electroencephalography (qEEG) – a measure of electrical activity in the brain

Randolph Attachment Disorder Questionnaire (RADQ) – a test assessing RAD

Reactive Attachment Disorder (RAD) – an inability to form healthy interpersonal relationships, arising from neglect, abuse, and/or abandonment within the early years of life

Referential Speaking – verbalizing praise to another adult about a youth within said youth's ear-shot

Reitan-Klove Fingertip Number Writing Test – a measure of tactile attention/sensation

Reitan-Klove Tactile Finger Recognition Test – a measure of tactile attention/sensation

Remeron – an anti-depressant medication (used to treat depression)

Restoril – an hypnotic medication (used to treat insomnia)

Risperdal – an atypical anti-psychotic medication (used to treat Borderline Condition/psychoses)

Ritalin – a psychostimulant medication (used to treat ADHD symptoms)

Rorschach Inkblot Technique – a projective psychometric test, helpful in diagnosing mental conditions

Sanguine – one of the four personality types, described as very social, extroverted, and talkative

Seashore Rhythm Test – a standardized measure of auditory attention/concentration and nonverbal acoustic analysis

Selective Norepinephrine Reuptake Inhibitor (SNRI) – a type of anti-depressant which allows the brain to better utilize the neurotransmitter Norepinephrine

Selective Serotonin Reuptake Inhibitor (SSRI) – a type of anti-depressant which allows the brain to better utilize the neurotransmitter Serotonin

Selective Verbal Learning Test – a measure of verbal memory

Sequelae – harmful results of a disorder or syndrome

Serax – an anxiolytic medication (used to treat anxiety)

Seroquel – an atypical anti-psychotic medication (used to treat Borderline Condition/psychoses)

Serotonin – one of several neurotransmitters in the brain

Serotonin Antagonist and Reuptake Inhibitor (SARI) – a type of anti-depressant which allows the brain to better utilize the neurotransmitter Serotonin, but different in chemical structure to SSRIs

Serzone – an SARI anti-depressant medication (used to treat depression)

Sinequan – an anti-depressant medication (used to treat depression)

Single Photon Emission Computerized Tomography (SPECT) –
    somewhat similar to PET, an imaging test used in neurology and
    psychiatry

Smiling Depression – an atypical depression, without the usual mani-
    festations of depression, typically used synonymously with
    masked depression and atypical depression

Soft-sign – a possible clue pointing to one or more specific disorders,
    often used somewhat synonymously with 'marker'

Somnolence – sleepiness

Soporific – a medication used to induce sleep

Speech Sounds Perception Test – a standardized measure of auditory-
    visual attention/concentration and phonetic speech analysis

Strattera – an SNRI anti-depressant medication (used to treat ADHD
    symptoms)

Stroop Color-Word Test – a standardized test measuring mental acuity
    and visual attention

Study Skills Program (SSP) – training in academic organizational
    skills, note-taking, etc

Super-ego Structure – conscience

Surrogate Adult – a child who plays the role of an adult in a relation-
    ship

Sustained Release – a medication in which the active ingredients are
    absorbed into the body at a consistent level

Synapse – the tiny space between nerve cells in the brain

Tack-On Phenomenon (TOP) – adding one psychotropic after another
    to a youth, without proper ongoing assessment

Tactile – the sense of touch

Tactile Finger Recognition Test – a measure of tactile attention and
    concentration

Teacher-Parent Conduit – teacher/parent communication

Tegretol – an anti-convulsant medication (used to treat Bipolar, seizure
    disorders, or impulse control syndromes)

Temporal Lobes – the part of the cerebrum which lies underneath the temples – involved in a host of complex cognitive capabilities

Temporo-parietal lobes – the region of the cerebrum encompassing both the temporal and parietal lobes

Tenex – a Beta-blocker medication (used to treat ADHD symptoms and/or Hypertension)

Test of Auditory Discrimination (TAD) – a standardized measure of auditory attention/concentration

Thematic Apperception Test (TAT) – a projective measure developed in the 1930s to assess personality structure

Thematic Apperception Test-Gray Adaptation (TAT-GA) – a measure assessing super-ego structure, emotionality, and subtle thought disorder

Thorazine – the very first neuroleptic medication, developed in 1953 (for treatment of psychoses)

Time-out – a disciplinary technique in which a child spends a specified amount of time in a specified place for a specified offense

Tofranil – a tricyclic anti-depressant medication (used to treat depression)

Topamax – an anti-convulsant medication (used to treat Bipolar, seizure disorders, or impulse control syndromes)

Toxic Verbal Gameyness – a youth's tendency to engage in a never ending debate with parents, for purposes of manipulation

Trail Making Test – a standardized measure assessing visual-spatial/visual-motor skills, as well as higher cognition

Trazodone – an anti-depressant medication (frequently used to treat insomnia)

Tricyclic Anti-depressants – the oldest group of mood elevating medications

Unresolved Anger – feelings of hostility which have yet to be dealt with

Valium – an anxiolytic medication (used to treat anxiety)

Verbal Scale Intelligence Quotient (VIQ) – a measurement of overall verbal abilities, from the Wechsler IQ tests

Visual-Motor – combining vision with motor skills

Visual-Spatial – combining vision with spatial skills

Wechsler Adult Intelligence Scale-3rd Edition (WAIS-III) – a standardized IQ test for adults

Wechsler Intelligence Scale for Children-3rd Edition (WISC-III) – a standardized IQ test for children and teens

Wechsler Preschool and Primary Scale of Intelligence-3rd Edition (WPPSI-III) – a standardized IQ test for preschool and Kindergarten youngsters

Wellbutrin – an anti-depressant medication (used to treat depression)

Wellbutrin SR – an anti-depressant medication, sustained release

Woodcock Johnson-Revised Edition (WJ-R) – a collection of standardized subtests measuring academic skills

Word Selective Reminding – a measure of verbal memory

Xanax – an anxiolytic medication (used to treat anxiety)

Zoloft – an SSRI anti-depressant medication (used to treat depression)

Zyprexa – an atypical anti-psychotic medication (used to treat Borderline Condition/psychoses)

Appendix III

Bibliography of Tests –
Gray Neuropsychology Associates, Inc.

Bender, L. *Bender Visual-Motor Gestalt Test*. Los Angeles, California: Western Psychological Services, 1938.

Dunn, L., & Dunn L. *Peabody Picture Vocabulary Test – Third Revision*. Circle Pines, Minnesota: American Guidance Service, 1997.

Exner, J. *A Rorschach Workbook for the Comprehensive System, 5th Ed*. Asheville, North Carolina: Rorschach Workshops, 2001.

Gilliam, J. *Gilliam Autism Rating Scale*. Austin, Texas: Pro-Ed, 1995.

Golden, C. *Stroop Color and Word Test*. Wood Dale, Illinois: Stoelting Company, 1978.

Goldman, R., Fristoe, M., & Woodcock, R. *Goldman-Fristoe-Woodcock Test of Auditory Discrimination*. Circle Pines, Minnesota: American Guidance Service, 1970.

Gordon, M. *The Gordon Diagnostic System*. DeWitt, New York: Gordon Systems, 1989.

Gray, S. *Attention Deficit Hyperactivity Weighting Scale.* Arlington, Texas: Gray Neuropsychology Associates, 1996.

Gray, S. *Gray Writing Samples Test.* Arlington, Texas: Gray Neuropsychology Associates, 1994.

Gray, S. *Thematic Apperception Test – Gray Adaptation.* Arlington, Texas: Gray Neuropsychology Associates, 1989.

Kaplan, E., Fein, D., Kramer, J., Delis, D., & Morris, R. "Coding – Incidental Learning Test," *Wechsler Intelligence Scale for Children III-PI.* San Antonio, Texas: The Psychological Corporation, Harcourt Brace Jovanovich, 1999.

Lachar, D., Wirt, R., Seat, P., & Broen, W., Jr. *Personality Inventory for Children.* Los Angeles, California: Western Psychological Services, 1981.

Littauer, F. *Littauer Personality Profile.* San Marcos, California: CLASS Book Service, 1983.

Murray, H. *Thematic Apperception Test.* Cambridge, Massachusetts: Harvard University Press, 1935.

Randolph, E. *Randolph Attachment Disorder Questionnaire.* Kittredge, Colorado: Institute for Attachment and Child Development, 1996.

Reitan, R. "Color-Form Test," *Halstead-Reitan Neuropsychological Battery.* Tempe, Arizona: Reitan Neuropsychology Laboratories, 1994.

Reitan, R. "Fingertip Number Writing Test of the Reitan-Klove Sensory-Perceptual Examination," *Halstead-Reitan Neuropsychological Battery.* Tempe, Arizona: Reitan Neuropsychology Laboratories, 1994.

Reitan, R. "Lateral Dominance Examination," *Halstead-Reitan Neuropsychological Battery*. Tempe, Arizona: Reitan Neuropsychology Laboratories, 1994.

Reitan, R. "Progressive Figures Test," *Halstead-Reitan Neuropsychological Battery*. Tempe, Arizona: Reitan Neuropsychology Laboratories, 1994.

Reitan, R. "Seashore Rhythm Test," *Halstead-Reitan Neuropsychological Battery*. Tempe, Arizona: Reitan Neuropsychology Laboratories, 1994.

Reitan, R. "Speech Sounds Perception Test," *Halstead-Reitan Neuropsychological Battery*. Tempe, Arizona: Reitan Neuropsychology Laboratories, 1994.

Reitan, R. "Tactile Finger Recognition Test," *Halstead-Reitan Neuropsychological Battery*. Tempe, Arizona: Reitan Neuropsychology Laboratories, 1994.

Reitan, R. "Trail Making Test," *Halstead-Reitan Neuropsychological Battery*. Tempe, Arizona: Reitan Neuropsychology Laboratories, 1994.

Reynolds, C., & Bigler, E. "Abstract Visual Memory," *Test of Memory and Learning*. Austin, Texas: Pro-Ed, 1994.

Reynolds, C., & Bigler, E. "Word Selective Reminding," *Test of Memory and Learning*. Austin, Texas: Pro-Ed, 1994.

Wechsler, D. *Wechsler Intelligence Scale for Children – III*. San Antonio, Texas: The Psychological Corporation Harcourt Brace Jovanovich, 1991.

Wechsler, D. *Wechsler Preschool and Primary Scale of Intelligence –
III*. San Antonio, Texas: The Psychological Corporation Harcourt
Brace Jovanovich, 2002.

Woodcock, R., & Johnson, M. *Woodcock-Johnson Tests of
Achievement – Revised: Standard and Supplemental Batteries*.
Allen, Texas: DLM Teaching Resources, 1989.

Bibliography

Amen, D. (1998). *Change Your Brain, Change Your Life: The Breakthrough Program for Conquering Anxiety, Depression, Obsessiveness, Anger and Impulsiveness.* New York, New York: Three Rivers Press.

Amen, D., & Routh, L. (2003). *Healing Anxiety and Depression: The Revolutionary Brain-Based Program That Allows You to See and Heal the 7 Types of Anxiety and Depression.* Itasca, Illinois: Putnam Publishing Group.

Berne, E. (1969). *Games People Play: The Basic Handbook of Transactional Analysis.* New York: Random House, Inc.

Blue, J. (2000). Cell Phone Therapy. Arlington, Texas: Gray Neuropsychology Associates, Inc.

Bush, G. (1990). Public communication.

Conroy, P., & Carlino, L. (1979). *The Great Santini.* Burbank, California: Warner Studios.

Cornale, M. (1992). Personal communication.

Dobson, J. (2004). *The New Strong-Willed Child: Birth Through Adolescence.* Wheaton, Illinois: Tyndale House Publishers.

EEG Spectrum (2003). www.eegspectrum.com. Encino, California.

Federici, R. (1998). *Help for the Hopeless Child: A Guide for Families.* Alexandria, Virginia: Ronald S. Federici and Associates.

Feifer, S., & De Fina, P. (2002). *The Neuropsychology of Written Language Disorders: Diagnosis and Treatment.* Middletown, Maryland: School Neuropsychology Press, LLC.

Gray, S. (1996). *Attention Deficit Hyperactivity Weighting Scale.* Arlington, Texas: Gray Neuropsychology Associates, Inc.

Gray, S. (2000). Audio Therapy. Arlington, Texas: Gray Neuropsychology Associates, Inc.

Gray, S., & Blue, J. (1999). Bland Sandwich Therapy. Arlington, Texas: Gray Neuropsychology Associates, Inc.

Gray, S. (1994). *Gray Writing Samples Test.* Arlington, Texas: Gray Neuropsychology Associates, 1994.

Gray, S. (2004). *The Maltreated Child: Finding What Lurks Beneath.* Colorado Springs, Colorado: Living Water Press.

Gray, S. (2005*). *The Menacing Child: Parent Survival Strategies.* Colorado Springs, Colorado: Living Water Press.   [*due out in 2005]

Gray, S. (1999). Toxic Verbal Gameyness. Arlington, Texas: Gray Neuropsychology Associates, Inc.

Gray, S. (2000). VideoCam Therapy. Arlington, Texas: Gray Neuropsychology Associates, Inc.

Gregorc, A. (1982). *An Adult's Guide to Style.* Columbus, Connecticut: Gregorc Associates.

Holley, D. (2003). Personal communication.

Kaye, K. (1994). *Family Rules*: *Raising Responsible Children.* New York, New York: St. Martin's Paperbacks.

LaHaye, T. (1993). *Spirit-Controlled Temperament*. Wheaton, Illinois: Tyndale House Publishers.

Littauer, F. (1983). *Littauer Personality Profile*. San Marcos, California: CLASS Book Service, 1983.

Littauer, F. (1992). *Personality Plus: How to Understand Others by Understanding Yourself*. Old Tappan, New Jersey: Fleming H. Revell Co.

Lubar, J., & Lubar, J. (1999). Neurofeedback Assessment and Treatment for Attention Deficit/Hyperactivity Disorders (ADD/HD). In J. R. Evans & A. Abarbanel (Eds), *Introduction to Quantitative EEG and Neurotherapy*. New York, New York: Academic Press.

Mandel, H., & Marcus, S. (1988). *The Psychology of Under-achievement: Differential Diagnosis and Treatment*. Hoboken, New Jersey: John Wiley & Sons.

Peale, N. (1987). *The Amazing Results of Positive Thinking*. New York, New York: Simon & Schuster.

Peterson, E. (1995). *The Message*. Colorado Springs, Colorado: NavPress Publishing Group.

Perot, R. (1992). Speech before the National Press Club. Washington, D.C.

Petti, T., & Vela, R. (1990). Borderline Disorders of Childhood: An Overview. *Journal of the American Academy of Child and Adolescent Psychiatry*, 29, 327-337.

Rimm, S. (1995). *Why Bright Kids Get Poor Grades: And What You Can Do About It*. New York: Crown Publishing.

Rourke, B. (1995). *Syndrome of Nonverbal Learning Disabilities*: *Neurodevelopmental Manifestations*. New York, New York: Guilford Publications, Inc.

Smalley, G., & Trent, J. (1990). *The Two Sides of Love*: *What Strengthens Affection, Closeness and Lasting Commitment*. Colorado Springs, Colorado: Focus on the Family.

Sterman, M., Macdonald, L., & Stone, R. (1974). Biofeedback Training of the Sensorimotor EEG Rhythm in Man: Effects on Epilepsy. *Epilepsia*, 15, 395-416.

Teaff, G. (1994). *Coaching In the Classroom*: *Teaching Self-Motivation*. Waco, Texas: Cord Communications.

Tobias, C. (1999). *Every Child Can Succeed: Making the Most of Your Child's Learning Style*. Colorado Springs, Colorado: Focus On the Family Publishing.

Walbrown, F., & Walbrown, J. (1990). *So Your Child Has a Learning Problem: Now What?*, *2nd Ed*. Brandon, Vermont: Clinical Psychology Publishing Company, Inc.

Whitley, M. (2001). *Bright Minds, Poor Grades*: *Understanding and Motivating Your Underachieving Child*. New York, New York: The Berkley Publishing Group.

Wilkes, G. (1998). *Jesus On Leadership*. Wheaton, Illinois: Tyndale House Publishers.

Index

Meet the Author

Steven G. Gray, Ph.D., a board certified pediatric neuropsychologist, is clinical director of Gray Neuropsychology Associates, Inc – with clinics in Texas and Colorado.

Dr. Gray's passion is helping young persons and their parents. Common childhood/adolescent disorders he treats include: Academic Underachievement Syndrome, ADHD, Learning Disabilities, Reactive Attachment Disorder, Borderline Condition, Oppositional Defiant Disorder, Childhood/Adolescence Bipolar Disorder, Conduct Disorder, Dysthymic Disorder, Post-traumatic Stress Disorder, and Intermittent Explosive Disorder.

For over two decades Dr. Gray has specialized in helping youth get *on-track*. Blending his 22 years of clinical experience with a unique sense of humor, Dr. Gray presents *down-in-the-trenches*, Biblically-based, practical information. He is a popular speaker at workshops and seminars throughout the United States as well as internationally. Dr. Gray has served as Clinical Assistant Professor at the University of Texas Southwestern Medical Center in Dallas since 1988.

He is also the author of *The Maltreated Child: Finding What Lurks Beneath. The Maltreated Child* dives into the various underlying root causes from which a given youth is suffering. Once the primary causes are found and dealt with, then the youngster is set free to be all that God has created him to be. *The Maltreated Child* also offers many effective strategies for attacking the underlying root causes for why a specific young person is struggling.

Dr Gray, his wife Debbi, and teen-age son Forrest live in Colorado Springs with Kelsey, their Yellow Lab, and Autumn, their Golden Retriever. In his spare time, Dr. Gray enjoys alpine skiing, golf, Southern Gospel vocal music, movies, and travel.

For additional information regarding books, seminars, and/or speaking engagements, please write or call

email: gray.matter@mindspring.com
phone: 719.487.1760
USPS: Gray Neuropsychology Associates, Inc.
1840 Deer Creek Road, Suite 103
Monument, CO 80132

www.grayneuro.com

Order Form

www.grayneuro.com

Fax Orders: fax a copy of this order form to 719/487-1755
Email Orders: gray.matter@mindspring.com
Postal Orders: Gray Neuropsychology Associates, Inc.
1840 Deer Creek Road, Suite 103, Monument, CO 80132

Please send me:

_____ copies of *Motivating Marvin: Helping Your Bright Underachiever Succeed in School* @ $20.00 ea. _____

_____ copies of *The Maltreated Child: Finding What Lurks Beneath* @ $25.00 ea. _____

6% sales tax (CO residents only): _____

5% Credit Card Service fee: _____

Shipping (see below): _____

Total Due: _____

Payment:

☐ Check   ☐ Visa   ☐ American Express
☐ Money Order   ☐ Mastercard   ☐ Discover
Credit Card orders: please add 5% to total cost

Credit card number: _____

Name on card:_____ Exp. Date: _____

Signature: _____

Ship to: _____

_____

_____

Shipping Rates:
   <u>Media Mail</u>: $ 3.00 per book   *(allow 3 to 10 days)*
   <u>Fed Ex</u>: $17.85 per book   *(guaranteed 2 day delivery)*

_____ I would like more information regarding an evaluation and/or EEG Neurofeedback treatment for my child/teen.